# SO, YOU WANT TO
## START A NONPROFIT,
# NOW WHAT?

*How to start and run a successful
501(c)(3) charitable organization*

By

## Michele L. Whetzel

TWIN WILLOWS
PUBLISHING

Published by Twin Willows Publishing, Newark, Delaware
ISBN: 979-8-218-19852-7

This book is dedicated to my husband, Robert Whetzel, and my children, Alexandra and Michael for always believing in me. You constantly shake your heads when I do the next crazy thing, but I hope I keep things fun and interesting for you. I love you all more than you could ever know. Thank you for your continued love and support.

# TABLE OF CONTENTS

———·•◉•·———

# INTRODUCTION

You may have picked up this book because you wish to **start a new nonprofit organization** to honor a loved one. They may have died tragically from illness, carelessness, or just plain lack of training, and you want to prevent this tragedy from happening to others. Or maybe you see a gaping hole that is not being addressed, and you feel you are the right person to start to fill that hole. Maybe you are just a caring soul who wants to share your gifts to lift others up and get them to a better place through compassion, mentoring, or financial support. I commend you for wanting to help others, and in this book, I will help you determine the best way to put your desires into practice to work toward your end goals.

You may be reading this book because you want to find better ways serve your community – by **improving your existing nonprofit or by learning how to be a more effective board member, nonprofit staff member, or executive director.** Maybe you feel the desire to be an entrepreneur and are thinking a nonprofit may be the way to go.

**Whatever your reason, this book will help you run a successful nonprofit organization that can last for generations – or until the need for your nonprofit's support has become obsolete.**

I have met many kind, ambitious people who have told me of their plans to start a nonprofit. They have seen a need, they want to fill a void, or they have some skills and talents they would like to share to help others. While their intentions are genuine and their aspirations are honorable, they may know very little about running a nonprofit or how to go about setting one up in a way that will lead to future success. There may be reasons that a new nonprofit is not the best approach. We will explore the options together.

I wrote this book to help you determine if starting a new nonprofit is the right path for you, and, if so, to teach you the best way to go about doing it. **The book begins by looking at what you need to know and do before starting a nonprofit, then**

**delves into what it takes to properly set up a 501(c)(3) public charity, and it finishes with how to sustain and grow your organization.** There is a wealth of information in the appendices, from a listing of nonprofit resource organizations in each state to a business plan outline, to help you along the way.

I live in Delaware where more than 50% of publicly-traded companies in the US and 60% of Fortune 500 companies are incorporated.[1] Throughout this book when I discuss incorporation and related topics, the information may be Delaware-centric, but I will also provide national and regional sources you can use for your local area.

In the process of writing this book, I interviewed more than 60 nonprofit experts. I will share their advice on how to create a successful nonprofit and how to avoid common pitfalls. We all want the program you have imagined to become your crowning achievement. You may also use the lessons learned here to coach others in their nonprofit ventures.

I have a varied background that includes running three statewide nonprofit organizations and serving on more than a dozen nonprofit boards. Through this service I received a great education in nonprofit governance and best practices along the way. I started two of the charitable organizations from just an idea by incorporating them, filing for 501(c)(3) status with the IRS, creating bylaws, forming a board, etc. – all of which I will teach you in this book.

I have also had to help shut down the operations of two nonprofits, so I will guide you through that difficult process, too. A nonprofit may no longer be serving its mission, or it may be that you need to shut down your organization because it has been so successful, the services are no longer needed.

If you like what you read here, please let others know by leaving a book review on the Amazon book page. On my website www.501Guide.com, **you will find sample bylaws and helpful policy and procedure samples** you can adapt for your organization. You may contact me at mlwhetzel@501Guide.com. I look forward to hearing your success stories!

---

[1] ("Business" [2018]) Delaware.gov https://delaware.gov/guides/business/

# PREFACE

————— ·•◉•· —————

The title of this book may suggest that it is written only for readers who are starting a new nonprofit. While the book is meant to help the reader who has an idea to start a new charitable organization, anyone who is involved with a nonprofit can find valuable information here.

*So, You Want to Start a Nonprofit, Now What?* is intended to assist a wide range of individuals who may be involved with nonprofit entities. Your role in the nonprofit community may change over time, so see below for some suggestions to use the book for your specific needs.

## Nonprofit Founder:

- Start with Chapters 1-3
- Continue with Chapters 4-8 if you decide starting a nonprofit is right for you
- Keep the book as a handy guide for future needs

## Board Members:

- Chapters 1, 2, 6, 7, 8, and 11 will give you a good base
- As the organization is evolving, Chapters 9 and 10 will come into play

## Nonprofit Executive Director:

- A lot will depend on the type of organization you join as the ED, but Chapters 1, 2, 6, 7, 8, and 11 will help guide you
- Use the book as a reference as needed

CHAPTER 1

# TEN MUST-HAVES FOR A
# SUCCESSFUL NONPROFIT

———·•●•·———

*"Sometimes it's the little things that are the big things."*

— Karla Lodholz
(Director of Resource Development & Member
Relations at Wisconsin Philanthropy Network)

It takes a village and more to start and run a successful nonprofit. This list of must-haves will not guarantee success, but without them success will not be easy. The chapters that follow will help put you, and keep you, on the path to success.

1. You will need unwavering **commitment** to your cause.

2. Fill an **unmet need** in a unique way for your area.

3. Do your **research** into what work is being done in your location, the need, if the community will get behind you, and funding options.

4. Create a **business plan** from the start and adapt as you grow and change.

5. Put together a **board** made up of passionate people who are committed to the mission and are diverse in expertise, thought, industry, age, race, background, and representative of the community you plan to serve. Because a nonprofit IS a business, there must also be members with business expertise.

6. Find **funding sources before you begin** and continue to search out new sources. (You cannot rely solely on family funds and resources.)

7. It is important to have **time to dedicate** to this passion project. Success will take more time and effort than a part-time job in most cases.

8. Rely on a **good support system**, including:
   - ○ Family involvement and/or support
   - ○ Mentor or trusted advisors
   - ○ Professionals (paid or volunteer) like a CPA and attorney who have prior nonprofit experience, accountant or bookkeeper, web designer, social media expert, IT services, grant writer

9. You must **be adaptable and have an ability to delegate.**

10. All of the above efforts will fail if not operating with **complete transparency and ethical practices**. People will forgive someone who has integrity if mistakes are made.

# CHAPTER 2

# WHAT IS A NONPROFIT?

————··●··————

*"Nonprofits exist to fill gaps,*
*not to be permanent crutches."*

— Logan Herring (CEO of WRK Group)

**T**he term 'nonprofit' means different things to different people. It's a commonly used word without a common understanding between writer and reader. People often use the words 'nonprofit' and 'tax exempt' interchangeably. Congress has created almost three dozen types of tax-exempt organizations in different sections of the tax code.

"Each section identifies certain conditions that must be met to be exempt from paying federal income taxes. The one common condition is not paying out profits ('no part of the organization's net earnings can inure to the benefit of any private shareholder or individual'); hence the term, 'nonprofit.' Section 501(c)(3) of the tax code refers to 'public charities' (also known as charitable nonprofits) and 'private foundations.' The tax code [also] considers 'churches and religious organizations' (which the IRS defines to include mosques, synagogues, temples, and other houses of worship) to be 'public charities.'"[2]

Nonprofits are all connected by the common mission of improving quality of life. They receive charitable resources that some in the community are contributing to with the purpose of benefitting others in the community. Nonprofits are the conduits of social investment, meaning the public invests in them with the expectation that the funds will be passed through the organization in a way that improves the community.

---

[2] **("America's Nonprofits" [2022]) National Council of Nonprofits** (Reprinted with permission from the National Council of Nonprofits.) https://www.councilofnonprofits.org/what-is-a-nonprofit

In many cases, they are filling the gaps that government would otherwise need to find a way to fill.

A public charity's nonprofit status is determined by the IRS, and it receives that tax-exempt status because it is meant to serve the public. It is exempt from paying federal corporate income taxes, and eligible contributions may be tax deductible for the donor.

The objective of a nonprofit should be to advance the purpose for which it has been recognized as tax-exempt rather than to make a profit. The public charity's profits are meant to go toward its mission and not to benefit any individual or private stakeholder, and it is meant to serve the public. That is not to say that there should be no paid staff or contractors, or that there should not be a substantial effort for the organization to make money. Future chapters will delve into these ideas further.

### Types of Nonprofits

**Appendix II lists all of the categories of IRS "501" nonprofits.** The IRS has dozens of types of nonprofit organization distinctions. There are only a few for which contributions are tax-deductible for the donors. This group of nonprofits makes up more than 70% of the over 1.7 million U.S. nonprofit organizations.[3] We rely on nonprofits to play an important social sector role.

Most charitable organizations the general public is familiar with are under the IRS 501(c)(3) category. These are entities that are organized and operated exclusively for religious, charitable, scientific, literary, or educational purposes, for testing for public safety, to foster national or international amateur sports competition, or for the prevention of cruelty to children, women, or animals. The 501(c)(3) exemption also applies for any non-incorporated community chest, fund, cooperating association or foundation organized and operated exclusively for those purposes, as well as supporting organizations—often referred to in shorthand form as "Friends of" organizations.[4]

Within the 501(c)(3) category, there are different types of 501(c)(3) nonprofit organizations. **The three main distinctions are private foundations, private operating foundations, and public charities.**

---

[3] ("The Nonprofit Sector in Brief" [2019]) National Center for Charitable Statistics Urban Institute https://nccs.urban.org/publication/nonprofit-sector-brief-2019#the-nonprofit-sector-in-brief-2019
[4] ("501(c)(3) organization" [2022]) Wikipedia https://en.wikipedia.org/wiki/501(c)(3)_organization

**Private foundations** do not have active programs, and they are meant to fund other organizations' programs. They usually have a small group of donors (or one wealthy donor) and will create an endowment fund that will live on in perpetuity to give to those organizations that further their mission. Often these foundations are started and run by family members. Family foundations make up more than half of all private (family, corporate, independent, and operating) foundations. A family foundation's funds are derived from members of a single family, but "family foundation" is not a legal term and has no precise definition. Usually one or more family members will serve as an officer or board member and may play a significant role in governing and/or managing the foundation. Because they almost always use the income from an endowment for grants, and endowments go on in perpetuity, many family foundations have second- and third-generation descendants of the original donors managing the foundation.[5]

**Private operating foundations** are much less common, and are similar to private foundations, but the difference is that they also have active programs like most public charities. Like private foundations, they receive their funding from non-public sources.

**Public charities**[6] are the most common type of 501(c)(3) nonprofit organization. They are eligible to receive tax-deductible donations from individuals (up to 50% of an individual donor's adjusted gross income) and corporations (up to 10% of the organization's revenue), and are governed by a board of directors. (California law requires that no more than 50% of the board members can be related to each other.) Public charities are expected to receive a substantial portion of their income from the public.

Within the public charity category, most organizations are operating nonprofits, meaning they offer programs to fulfill their mission. Some, however, are grant-making charities that do not actively run their own programs, but they raise funds to distribute to operating public charities to carry out their mission. To further complicate things, a public charity may use the word "foundation" in its corporate name, even if it is a public charity that receives most of its funding from the public and runs its own programs.

---

[5] ("Family Foundations" [2022]) Council on Foundations https://www.cof.org/foundation-type/family-foundations

[6] ("Understanding the Different Types of 501(c)(3) Non-Profit Organizations" [2015]) QuickBooks Blog https://quickbooks.intuit.com/r/starting-a-business/understanding-the-different-types-of-501c3-non-profit-organizations/

This book will focus specifically on public charities in the United States under section 501(c)(3) of the Internal Revenue Code, and "nonprofit" means a public charity unless stated otherwise.

## Different Structures and Arrangements

There are hundreds, if not thousands, of variations of operational structures within the public charity realm. **Here are a few of the different types of organizations I have been a part of over the past 20+ years (all are 501(c)(3) public nonprofits):**

1. An organization with the vision that "the poor should never be treated poorly" was started in 1979 by a young Capuchin Franciscan friar who moved to Wilmington, Delaware and saw a need for a soup kitchen for low-income and unhoused people. Brother Ronald still heads up the charity, and it has now grown to include three dining rooms, five emergency shelters, three childcare centers, three affordable housing senior living facilities, a collection and distribution center, a job placement center, a dental office, and a mobile health outreach van. All of this is run by a very strong board, a large staff at dozens of locations throughout the city, an advisory council, a guild board that helps with fundraisers, and many other volunteers.

2. A nonprofit hybrid where the tax-exempt organization collects donated items and cash donations from donors (the public) to give out to those in need, while the state provides the salaries for the two employees and the office space and equipment, so there is very little overhead.

3. An all-volunteer organization with the original goal of getting 1,000 donors to each give $1,000 to create an endowment, with the earnings from the endowment being granted annually to fund women's and girls' programs in Delaware.

4. An organization that started with an idea to gift leftover tickets to local sporting events, plays, and other public events to foster families, so they would be able to have experiences they would otherwise be unable to afford. This charity started as a family operation. The family and board grew it to where it now has ten staff members, with the original founder still leading the organization. It now offers a number of different programs for kids in the foster care system, especially those just entering the system and those about to age out.

5. A community foundation with a mission to improve the lives of Delaware residents by empowering and growing philanthropy that now has $344 million under management and helps the community in myriad ways.

6. Originally serving neglected and abused boys in a group home setting in the 1960s, the organization then grew to provide services for the entire family, and it now offers all types of services for victims of abuse or neglect, a domestic violence hotline, shelters, and parenting education. It has a board and dozens of staff members working in different locations in the state.

7. A steering committee with the mission of finally getting an equal rights amendment passed in our country and in the state of Delaware.

8. An invitation-only membership organization (see ARCS Foundation below) started and run by women who aid advancement in science and technology by sponsoring specific American students at top research universities. Funds are raised through member dues, individual and corporate underwriters, and volunteer work. (I have been a member of the Washington, DC Chapter since 2016.)

## ARCS Foundation

The Achievement Awards for College Scientists (ARCS) Foundation was started in 1958 by a group of philanthropic women in California who saw the space race heating up when the Soviet Union launched the Sputnik satellite the previous year. That event both fascinated and alarmed Americans. These women strongly believed they could make a difference for our country by funding college scholarships for American science students.

Because they were initially focused on contributing to the American space program, they also started Houston, Texas and Washington, DC chapters in addition to the California chapter. They established strong relationships and raised funds through member dues, individual donations, and corporate sponsorships. They used these funds to support the science scholars at the schools in the chapter areas.

This is an all-volunteer nonprofit organization that has now grown to more than 1,200 members and 15 chapters in areas across the country where there are universities with strong science programs. They have provided more than 10,000 students of science with awards totaling more than $120 million.

The organization has remained strong because its mission is simple, and it continues to look at ways to perfect the model. There is a national board that works closely with the local chapters. "National" provides the branding and common messaging while the 15 local chapters each operate individually and uniquely to form great relationships with their local universities and funded scholars. They then communicate back to the national group with ways in which the umbrella organization can help. There is also a national advisory council of people in the scientific arena.

Each chapter organization receives advice from national and other chapters on how best to run their boards and attract new members, but with each being in a different location, they will find that what works for them may not work in a different region. Chapters differ in the amount they charge for membership, the scholarship award amounts, and the number of years they will fund a scholar with a single grant. They work with the local universities and members to see what makes sense for their organization.

As with most successful nonprofits, there is a strong committee network. In this case, in addition to chapter committees, they also have national committees with representatives from each chapter so they can discuss universal problems and get ideas for solutions.

9. An all-volunteer organization with no physical headquarters that has been in existence for more than 25 years with a mission to give scholarships to women in Delaware who want to improve their lives and the lives of their families by finally obtaining their undergraduate degrees.

10. An all-volunteer affiliate of a national umbrella organization (at a New Jersey university) that organizes classes to help women prepare to run a political campaign. The aim is to get more women involved in the political process.

All of the above are public charities. There are also 501(c)(3) organizations that include hospitals, schools, and groups that are working to save our planet. For some local branches of larger national organizations (somewhat like a franchise of a national for-profit organization), the local affiliate may owe dues to the national organization for use of the name and other resources. You can see, there is quite an array of options.

There are approximately 1,000 public charities in the small state of Delaware. The state has about one million residents, so there is roughly one public charity for every 1,000 residents. Collectively, they are the number one employer in the state.

There are more than 1.7 million public charities in the United States. Many have overlapping missions and are competing for the same donor and grant dollars. A little research will reveal the nonprofits that exist in your area and what communities they serve.

## Founder Types & Motivations

There are generally three different groups of people who consider starting a nonprofit. The first group is comprised of those who have experienced a tragedy and have lost, or have come close to losing, a family member or close friend. They want to honor that person, and they seek ways to prevent others from going through the same tragedy. This may be by finding a cure for the rare disease. They may want to educate the public on ways to diagnose and treat early. Maybe they want to offer help for or prevent mental health, substance, eating disorder, or other issues. The people in this first group want to turn tragedy into triumph.

The next group is made up of people who have worked in and around the nonprofit sector and have recognized a hole or unfilled need they feel qualified to rectify, cure, or otherwise fix. They are passionate about serving the people (or animals) in the community, righting the wrongs, and trying to fix what is broken.

The third group contains those who have a talent they want to share, want to help others while sharing their talent, and believe starting a nonprofit would marry the two while also giving them paid employment. They may believe that if they start a nonprofit, they can easily find grants that will not only pay for the services they will be offering, but will also pay their salary. If you are in this group, you will find that there may be a better and easier way for you to successfully make a living AND make a difference.

# CHAPTER 3

# SHOULD YOU START A NEW NONPROFIT?

————·•●•·————

*"Do your little bit of good where you are; it's those little bits of good put together that overwhelm the world."*

Desmond Tutu

### The Founder Has to Be All-In

Renee[7] had a dream to start and run an organization that would offer out-patient support in her local area for people suffering with an eating disorder. Renee had struggled with disordered eating herself for years. She had twice gone to in-patient facilities in far-away states to find help and support. Each time when she returned to her home state, she found it very difficult to maintain all that she had gained from the in-patient facilities because she did not have a local organization to turn to for support. She had looked for options and found none, so she was determined to help other people like herself.

First, Renee entered her idea in a statewide entrepreneurial idea competition. Her plan was to create a permanent facility to address eating disorders in her area. Within a 24-hour period, her competition team put together a business plan, created a fully-functioning website, and sent out a survey to assess the need in the local community. Renee's team won the state competition and went on to compete in the global battle where the idea did very well against the competition.

---

[7] Throughout this book, names may have been changed to protect the privacy of the individuals who share their experience.

Renee received a lot of publicity about the contest, and the completed surveys showed there really was a need in the area, so Renee decided to ride the wave of support to start putting her plan into motion. Knowing it would be a while before a physical structure could be built, Renee decided to start her organization as a nonprofit that would provide resource tools and support for the people in her area, with a website and contact information to help them make connections. She put together a passionate board of friends and colleagues, including some who had a lot of nonprofit experience and contacts in her area. At its peak, the nonprofit had twelve board members and eight advisory council members.

They formed a corporation and applied for and received 501(c)(3) status from the Internal Revenue Service (IRS). A domain name was obtained and a new website was created, and all was up and running. They created vision and mission statements, bylaws, a logo, a brochure to share with physicians and others who may encounter those with disordered eating, business cards, a checking account, social media accounts, a dedicated phone number, and a PayPal account to more easily collect donations. All of these things happened in the fast-moving first four months of the organization's existence. It seemed like this nonprofit was on fire and was really going to make a difference!

Unfortunately, Renee, as the founder and leader of the organization, was also juggling a full-time job and a young family. Board meetings became fewer and further between, and the organization did not have enough momentum to remain sustainable. All board members were depending on the founder to set the pace. The organization needed to continue paying for the website, domain name, and the annual state taxes, and the funds they had were quickly being spent on these operational items that were not advancing the organization's mission. Four years after it began, Renee made the hard choice to dissolve the nonprofit. She hopes to be able to continue to help those suffering with eating disorders in other ways going forward.

Starting and running an independent nonprofit organization takes a considerable amount of time, energy, expertise, funding, and other resources – both to start it up and to maintain and grow it. Before you jump in with both feet, you are wise to weigh your options. You may find that, rather than starting and running a public charity, there are other ways to fulfill your mission that will better use your resources and talent.

There are a lot of good reasons to start a nonprofit. To do it right, you need to lay the foundation, and, with the proper passion and purpose, it can be done well. Running a nonprofit organization can be more difficult than running a small business, and there is a lot to take into consideration.

You should weigh and consider many factors before taking the plunge to start a new nonprofit. Many who have been there say the thing that most surprised them was how much effort and time went into the operations and administration of the organization, which took time away from the mission and goals. If you are passionate about a cause, consider the following before going through the steps of creating a new organization.

- **What is your "Why"?**
  - What are your reasons for wanting to start a nonprofit?
  - Make sure you want to do this for the right reasons – to fill a gap in services or awareness in a given area, to bring about the change you are passionate about – not to focus on your need for a job or to boost your ego.
- **What makes your organization unique?**
  - If you are the only one in your area providing this service and the service is needed, it may be easier to raise money to support it.
  - If you are duplicating work that is already being done in the local area, you will need to find ways for your program to stand out by finding a way to do it better or to fill holes in the existing structure. Are there problems with the existing service that you intend to improve or fix? Sometimes duplicated effort is not compounded and increased effort – it is diluted effort – so you should be sure there is a need for your new program.
- **Have you done your homework?**
  - Check to see **which organizations are doing similar work**, talk to them, and maybe shadow them to see what services they are providing.
  - Do a **feasibility study** by meeting with people in the community to be sure those you intend to serve believe this is a needed service, and to determine the level of need. If you are coming from a place of saviorism, swooping in to rescue a community that does not feel the need to be rescued, the program may not work.
  - Is there **data to prove there is a problem**, and how will your solution create a meaningful impact or solve that problem?

- Will your program(s) **"give a man a fish" or "teach him to fish?"** There are many unhoused or unemployed people who will not be helped solely by giving them a home or a job. Often there are countless underlying issues preventing them from being able to be self-sustaining. It would help them to make long-term gains if the multiple layers holding them back are addressed and treated.

- Consider **what is going on in the broader community, in the country, and/or in the world**, and whether these factors will have an effect on what you are trying to do. The 2007-2009 recession affected the income of many businesses in the country, and the pandemic from 2020-2022 made it difficult to deliver in-person services.

- **Determine if the larger community cares** enough about this cause to get behind your organization. There is so much competition for resources (funding and volunteers) that if your nonprofit is not a priority, you will be constantly running behind other organizations in seeking time, talent, and treasure.

- **Talk to grantors, individual donors**, and people who provide contracting services to nonprofits to assess your idea.
  - They will ask the hard questions that may cause you to redefine your plan.
  - Ask them if they would consider funding the program, what they would recommend, and what you should be thinking about.

- **Create a business plan**. (See Chapter 4 and Appendix III for business plan specifics.) A nonprofit IS a type of business and has many of the same tasks and concerns.
  - Will your business plan be allowed under IRS nonprofit requirements?
  - Do you have the business expertise to run it? If not, do you have others on your team who do?

- Prepare your "**elevator speech**" with your top three points of why and how you plan to run the nonprofit. If you have a heart-wrenching story, that may be all you need for some to sign on with you or fund you, but for business-minded people or foundation grants, you will need to be able to quickly and clearly articulate your top three points and drive them home a second time if you get the opportunity.

- If your organization is going to be part of a larger network (like a national or international organization), **check with the overarching organization** to be sure you have fulfilled all of their requirements.

- **Funding Considerations**:
  - ○ Are you comfortable with fundraising? As the founder, you will be the face of the organization and will be the main person raising funds in the early years.
    - ■ First you will be asking your core group of friends and family members.
    - ■ Later you will need to be fearless and passionate in branching out to convince others to buy into your mission and to help fund it.
  - ○ Determine if you could raise two to three years of estimated operating expenses right from the start. Many of the infrastructure-related costs will be the same whether your organization is large or small.
  - ○ You need to have some funding sources in place from the start, but check those sources to ensure they have an upstanding reputation and positive past history. Do not accept funds that could shine a negative light on your organization.
  - ○ Look at the IRS regulations regarding a 501(c)(3) to see if your startup funds would be diversified enough. The **IRS's Public Support Test**[8] requires that a public charity's income comes from a diverse set of donors (at least 1/3 from contributions from the general public unless other qualifications are met), figured over a 5-year period that will start in year 6 of a new nonprofit.
  - ○ Be sure you have the utmost ethical intentions and that you or your family members or close associates are not going to personally benefit from the nonprofit. Be very transparent from the start to avoid even the appearance of impropriety.
  - ○ Know that with a nonprofit, you are raising money to accomplish your mission (as opposed to running a business where you know that the ultimate mission is to bring in money). You have to always be selling that mission and need to believe in it fervently now and in the future. If you don't believe in the mission, potential funders will not be convinced to get behind it.
  - ○ Determine if there are public funds that could be put toward solving this issue.

---

[8] ("Advance Ruling Process Elimination – Public Support Test" [Updated October 5, 2022]) IRS.gov https://www.irs.gov/charities-non-profits/charitable-organizations/advance-ruling-process-elimination-public-support-test

○ Visit **IRS.gov** to review the instructions for filing a **Form 990**, the annual tax return for a nonprofit. You also may want to read through an existing nonprofit's filed 990 form to understand the filing requirements for your organization. (If you are starting small, in the early years the full 990 will not be required.)

○ Can you **attract a board** that will not only contribute time, talent, and treasure, but that will actively help you bring in new fundraising sources and will fulfill their fiduciary duties[9] to the organization? (More about this in Chapter 6: Board's First Steps.)

○ Be prepared to have an **ongoing commitment** to this cause for many years to come.

   ○ You will need to sacrifice your time and other resources for at least the first few years to be sure all is up and running smoothly.

   ○ If your nonprofit is created in response to a friend's or family member's tragedy (illness, suicide, other mental health or disability issue, or negligence), know that you will be revisiting that tragedy many times, and it may take you through an emotional quagmire each time you retell the story. Also, you, as the founder (and survivor of the tragedy) may be the one always in demand because it is your personal story.

   ○ Be sure your family is also committed and supportive because the time you put into the organization will inevitably take time away from them, or they may also be alongside you putting in sweat equity.

♦ **Try to determine if this need will exist five to ten years from now.**

   ● Will your organization become obsolete quickly? If so, you will need to find a way to pivot to stay relevant when that happens. Instead, you may want to consider an alternative way to meet your short-term goal that will not require the investment of time and energy running a nonprofit requires.

   ● Is your plan to fix a specific problem so you are able to put yourself out of business? If so, you will want to make that part of your mission.

---

[9] ("The Fiduciary Responsibilities of a Nonprofit Board of Directors" by Nick Price [March 12, 2018]) BoardEffect https://www.boardeffect.com/blog/fiduciary-responsibilities-nonprofit-board-directors/

♦ **Most nonprofits start as small grassroots organizations**, and many stay that way for a long time. They do not bring in enough revenue to pay salaries or consultants. Consider that your organization may be all-volunteer for quite a while.

♦ **Know that there will, in some ways, be more scrutiny** if you are a nonprofit vs. a for-profit entity. The IRS is giving nonprofits a pass on having to paying taxes, so they want to be sure nonprofits are following the IRS's rules. Also, the Form 990 for a nonprofit is publicly available, so the finances of the organization can be seen by anyone.

## There May Be an Alternative

Consider that there may be another way to have a successful program and fulfill your charitable ambition without all that is required to start and run a stand-alone public charity. There are many ways to interact with the nonprofit sector and have an impact. Here are some alternatives:

● If you do not have nonprofit experience, look to **join a board or committee** of an organization you believe in before committing fully to your own organization.

● There are times that, in order to be eligible for certain types of funding, your program will need to be a 501(c)(3) – on its own or under an existing nonprofit. Rather than going through the paperwork and filings required to start your own nonprofit, you may want to find a **fiscal sponsor** - an existing nonprofit or community foundation, that is willing to host your project under its 501(c)(3) umbrella. If your project is small or temporary, this will provide the tax-exempt status without the overhead and government filings needed for a stand-alone nonprofit. This will allow you to focus on your mission without having to spend a lot of time on the operations and will have your project up and running quickly.

For donations to be tax-deductible to the donor, all funds must go through the sponsoring organization. A contract will spell out the responsibilities of each side of the transaction for the fiscal sponsor and the project. If your project grows significantly or morphs into a larger program, you can look into going out on your own at that point. By then, you will have more of an idea what it will take to run an independent nonprofit organization and will have built up a network to help.

- Consider **partnering with an existing nonprofit** to create a program for its organization. You may be able to arrange to retain control of the project and may even be asked to join its board. You can put all of your work toward your mission and will not need to worry as much about the business aspects. This could save a lot in administrative costs.

- Open a **fund** at a local community foundation that is **donor-directed** or **donor-advised** to provide funds to a cause near and dear to your heart.

- **Organize a movement** and put together a group of like-minded individuals to fight for the thing you are passionate about. This could be run more like a club and does not need the corporate or nonprofit structure to be successful in creating the change you desire.

- Start a **for-profit company** and apply for **B Corp** certification. This is not a type of incorporation, but is a certification, and any corporation may apply. Unlike traditional for-profit corporations, B Corps are driven by both mission AND profit. They are accountable to their shareholders to produce a financial profit while also providing some sort of public benefit. For example, companies that donate one item to those in need for each item sold to the public are following the B Corp model.

- Similarly, a for-profit company could have a **charitable subsidiary** to which it funnels some of its profits.

- Start a **corporation that does fundraisers** for a particular charity or funds a different charity with the proceeds of each event.

  a. Create a separate, incorporated entity with its own bank account that is separate from your personal accounts. Check with an attorney or accountant who is well-versed in this type of entity to see if an LLC or other type of corporation will best fill your needs.

  b. Put together an invitation contact list that you can grow over time. The invitations could all be sent via email.

  c. Organize fundraising events, and announce the charitable recipient on the invitations – you could do one event a year, monthly, or every few months depending on your community's response. You need to get the approval of the charity ahead of time. Most will welcome your support, but they may have guidelines for those using their name to fundraise on their behalf.

  d. Invite a person from the receiving nonprofit to attend to give an elevator speech about the organization to those in attendance.

e. Charge a fee to attend, deduct the event expenses from the revenue, then donate the entire remaining balance to the charity of your choice.

f. Because all proceeds are donated, the organization has no income. The only expense is the state franchise tax (if you are the registered agent and it is applicable) and maybe the digital and email marketing platform you use to create and send invitations.

g. If you choose to invite people to your events without requiring some sort of membership to your group, there is no need for member management, bylaws, etc. People may choose to attend when they are available without any strings attached. (Also, if you set the organization up as a membership organization, you would be competing with other membership organizations.)

- Find a way to **prop up an existing nonprofit** that is already doing the work you are passionate about by raising funds. Some options:

  a. Social media fundraiser campaign

  b. Crowd funding page

  c. Email campaign to people who are passionate about the same cause

  d. "In lieu of flowers…" donations directly to an existing organization in remembrance of a loved one

  e. Organize a fundraising event and donate the proceeds

## Ready, or Not?

Ask yourself multiple times if you really need to start a new nonprofit to accomplish your goals. Of course, if you start with one of the above alternative options, you may organically grow into a nonprofit in time.

Starting a new nonprofit can be a Sisyphean task that can feel endless and futile at times, so be sure you are prepared for those hard times. Building an organization from scratch requires a lot of intellectual, physical, and emotional stamina.

Though your reason for starting a nonprofit is your passion for the mission, know that much of your time will be spent on day-to-day operations (fundraising, governance, social media posts, required filings, hiring, and HR), so you will need to find others to work on serving the mission while you are busy with these tasks, or vice versa. In time you may need staff or volunteers to work on locating funding options. Those who have been there will tell you they never expected how much time would be devoted to the operations and administrative side of the organization.

Of course, it is possible to start a small grassroots nonprofit organization with the intention of keeping it small. If it is a registered charity, no matter how small, there are still requirements to maintain the 501(c)(3) status.

In addition to having a passionate founder, the **three pillars** holding up any successful nonprofit are:

- Funding sources
- People to do the daily work
- Community support

Without all three of these, it will be difficult to find success. The daily "worker bees" need to be passionate about the cause and dedicated to furthering the mission, while the community support will come if the community understands and values the mission, and they will spread the word about your organization. The funding will come if the work is being done well and the good word is being spread.

Lastly, consider what it would take to shut down the nonprofit if you find that, although your passion for the cause does not wane, beyond your most Herculean efforts you are not able to keep the charity running. Chapter 12 of this book will go through the steps of dissolving a nonprofit - also not an easy feat.

There is a growing recognition of the importance of **nonprofits** in our society to provide aid where the **private** and **government/public** systems are not able. Our society is reliant on all three sectors to function well.

If you are ready to learn how to successfully run a nonprofit, read on!

# CHAPTER 4

# APPLYING YOUR VISION

————·•●•·————

*"Leaders are limited by their vision rather than*
*by their abilities."*

Roy T. Bennett
(author of *The Light in the Heart*)

So, you want to start a nonprofit...now what?

Now that you have determined that the best course for your passion is to start a new nonprofit, let's look at where you should start. Your formation strategy will inform a lot of the organizational culture from the start. The goal is to set up a great structure that can grow and evolve into a self-sustaining organization. As the founder of the organization, recognize that there will be a learning curve. Go into this adventure with a willingness to learn.

Your youth, inexperience, and/or strong ego may actually help you to create something that has never been created before. You may not know all that has been tried before and failed, so a dose of unbridled self-confidence may be just what is needed to make this nonprofit and its mission a success. Temper your confidence with some humility, though. Be willing to admit that you do not know how to do all that you intend to do, and seek out those who have that knowledge to fill your gaps.

You may go through this book's steps in any order that makes the most sense for your nonprofit. I am listing them in the order that I have done them with the public charities I have assisted. Your mission may need to be put on hold for a while as you set up the structure of the organization that will be the foundation for your future.

## Yoga for Seniors

A young woman, Stephanie*, met with a staff member, Louise*, at a local nonprofit support organization because Stephanie wanted to start a new nonprofit. She said she loves yoga, and yoga has been proven to be good for older adults, so she thought she could get grants to start a nonprofit to teach yoga to seniors.

Louise asked if Stephanie had done any research to see if there may already be some organizations offering physical activities for seniors – maybe senior centers, YMCAs, or even fitness or yoga centers. She had not. Louise then asked what Stephanie knew about nonprofits. She said she knew nothing.

Louise went on to explain that "nonprofit status" is actually a tax status, and the reason an organization is designated by the IRS as a nonprofit is because that organization has pledged to give all funds raised back to the mission of serving the community. A 501(c)(3) nonprofit organization is required to have a board of directors to run it. Stephanie would need to have a board that would vote to pay her (or not), and they would also vote on whether to hire her in the first place. Even though Stephanie would be the founder of the organization, the board makes the decisions, so they could choose to hire someone else.

There are many important differences between a nonprofit and a for-profit organization, but, just like a for-profit business, the nonprofit will have to pay employment taxes and follow employment laws for any of its employees. It will need to protect anyone who is making decisions by having insurance, have the ability to track the money, and to file reports to prove that funds have been used appropriately. Louise told Stephanie that she will need to raise money to pay for all of these other things, and those funds will not go directly toward the desired mission.

Stephanie learned that funders may love your mission, but rarely do they want to pay for computers, copiers, or insurance, so you have to find a way to raise even more money to pay for all of the overhead costs. Maybe she could test her idea by running her program through an existing nonprofit first. They may share some of their resources to help keep the costs down, and she would not be burdened with the extra work it takes to put together a board, incorporate, raise operating funds, etc.

Stephanie was uninformed, believing that nonprofits can get grant funding just because they exist. She was imagining the nonprofit could provide a salary for her while doing something she enjoys AND helping seniors at the same time. Win-win, right? Not so fast!

\* The names have been changed for this story.

Do your homework, make a solid plan, and start with the building blocks needed to create a strong foundation.

**Create a Business Plan\***

The business plan should include[10]:

1. An executive summary of the overall mission and plan
2. A description of the problem you intend to solve and for whom
3. Who your potential competitors are and why funders should choose your organization over them (why you are unique)
4. How you intend to reach your target recipient and funder audiences
5. An initial budget
6. Where you expect early funding to come from
7. How you plan to measure success
8. Any key risks and/or assumptions
9. Who will be managing the operations
10. With whom you are collaborating
11. Who is already committed

**\* Appendix III offers more business plan resources.**

**Decide on a Name**

Deciding what to name your organization is one of the most important decisions you will make. The name will be the first impression most people have of the nonprofit and will most likely remain the name as long as it exists.

---

[10] ("How to Write a Nonprofit Business Plan" [Updated for 2022]) Bplans https://articles.bplans.com/how-to-write-a-nonprofit-business-plan/

**Some things to consider in choosing a name:**

- Think big! Your first thought may be to name the organization after the program you are starting. Think about how that original name may constrict you when things really take off and you expand the programming you offer. For example, you name your nonprofit "Girls Can Do Anything," but years down the road your board decides you should also offer empowerment classes for boys. Why not start with a broader concept from the start, and call it "Can Do Anything," so you are not boxed in later.

- You may want to stay away from names that are specific to a place – if you are starting on Main Street and therefore name your nonprofit Main Street Services, what happens when you outgrow that space or you decide not to renew your lease there?

- If you are considering a name with a twist from the conventional spelling, or if the word has multiple spellings, will online searches be able to find you?

- You can adopt additional names if that suits your purpose. For a nominal fee you can file a Doing Business As (DBA) form with the state where you are incorporated (or, in some cases, with the local government where you are operating) and at the bank where your accounts are held. This means the overall umbrella organization will have the more general, all-encompassing name, but if you want to be able to accept payments and donations made to a more specific program name, you can do that, too. You may have more than one DBA if you choose. Your corporate name could be "XYZ Charity Fund" and your DBA name "Girls Can Do Anything."

- Do an online search for the name you are considering. Search for the "name only" to see any similarly-named organizations that exist. Again, think big! You will be starting out small and local, but someday you may be in direct competition with these organizations that had the name before you did.

- Next, do a search of the name and add your town or area to see what the local name competition may be. If you find organizations with a similar name but are in a completely different type of business, it may be alright to use that name for your nonprofit. Try to avoid names that may be confusingly similar to another organization, or you may find yourself in a legal dispute.

- Do a search for a domain name (a unique online address for a website). Run the words of the name you are considering together (no spaces between them) or add underscores between the words and add ".org," ".net," ".com," or other top-level domains (TLDs). (The majority of nonprofits use ".org" or ".net.")

Think about making it short and sweet so users can easily find and remember your Uniform Resource Locator (URL).

Sites like GoDaddy.com (a good example of a short, sweet, and memorable URL) will let you search for available names. Some of the more common names will already be owned, and the owners may be willing to sell you that name. It is worthwhile to secure your name as soon as possible, and the cost of the domain may influence the organization name you choose. There is more about domain names in Chapter 5.

- A Delaware corporation must include one of these words in its name: "association," "company," "corporation," "club," "foundation," "fund," "incorporated," "institute," "society," "union," "syndicate," or "limited," or an abbreviation of one of the above: https://icis.corp.delaware.gov/Ecorp/NameReserv/NameReservation.aspx. Check with the state in which you plan to incorporate to confirm its corporate naming requirements.

- If you choose a name that an existing organization feels is a threat to their competitive advantage or their reputation, they may come after you (you – the new, small guy) to force you to change your name. Even if it is your personal given name, they may force you to change your organization's name if they can prove they had that name first, they are well-known for that name, and your organization using the same name may cause harm to their organization. This could lead to legal fees to defend the suit and possibly fees to change your logo, signage, and incorporation or DBA, so it is better to foresee these obstacles and steer clear of them.

- You can file for a registered trademark on your organization's name to protect it from competitors going forward – if you are willing to go through the paperwork and extra cost. There are companies that specialize in helping you do this, or you can fill out the paperwork through the United States Patent and Trademark Office (www.uspto.gov/trademarks).

## Other Steps & Considerations

- Each state has its own **laws regulating what a nonprofit can do**, what it must do to be a legal nonprofit entity in that state, and how it may operate. No matter where you are formed, you need to follow state laws in any state where you solicit funding, and you may be required to register in each state.

- Find a successful nonprofit in your area and ask to **shadow the leader** of the organization for a few days. Even if its sector differs from yours, you will gain valuable insights into what the leader's job entails, the person's leadership style that has helped the organization to be successful, and what the job consists of on a day-to-day basis. Be sure to take notes on practices you want to adopt and use in your own soon-to-be-successful nonprofit.

- Decide on your **organization's formal structure**. If you set it up the right way at the beginning, it will help you down the line when applying for grants. Foundations and other grantors look first at whether you have obtained 501(c)(3) nonprofit status from the IRS, and then at whether you are following nonprofit best practices, have at least two years' funding in the bank, whether you have additional funding sources, who is on your board, and how well your organization is functioning. We will look more in detail at best practices, governance, and finances in future chapters.

- Because dotting the I's and crossing the T's is so imperative in these early stages, you may want to **hire or recruit professionals** like a CPA and an attorney to help you prepare the Certificate of Incorporation (aka Nonstock Charter) which is required in some states (see the sample in **Appendix IV**), obtain your Employer ID Number (EIN), create a corporation by filing with the state, and applying for 501(c)(3) status with the IRS. (Chapter 5 will cover this in more detail.) In some cases, these professionals may be willing to assist on a pro bono (no fee) basis. Be sure the professionals helping you have plenty of experience in the nonprofit sector. (Most of the above items can be done less expensively by the founder or a competent volunteer.)

- You are now the face of this new organization. Be sure to **clean up your personal social media pages!** Potential funders, volunteers, board members, and others will search online to learn more about you and your organization. You do not want to lose great prospects due to a questionable post from ten years ago.

- Put together a **peer network** by making connections with others in similar organizations, foundations (long before asking them for a grant), local officials, and others in leadership roles in the community you wish to serve. This network will help guide you and get the word out about your organization. Some may become board members, mentors, funders, or cheerleaders for you and your organization. Being a nonprofit leader can be lonely at times – you don't want to continually complain to the board, and you don't want to worry your employees or create uncertainty among the staff members if you voice concerns to them. Talking to other nonprofit leaders can be beneficial. Collegial support can garner advice or can just be a group to lean on and think out loud with.

- Remember, as the founder/leader of the organization, you need to **take care of yourself** and your own relationships at the same time you are taking care of the organization. Executive burnout is an all-too-real disorder, so you want to find outlets for stress and concerns. Regular exercise, a peer network to confide in, and other self-care rituals will help stave off burnout.

- Determine your organization's **Value Proposition** – what the organization values and why a potential funder should give to you rather than another organization or not at all. This is not your mission statement, but rather a donor-centric message that is clear and sets your nonprofit's work apart from others', helping them understand why they should want to give. The Value Proposition should be tied to your organization's mission rather than being a very general statement that could apply to any nonprofit, and the values should be reflected in your day-to-day practices. They need to be held so deeply, you are willing to give up work or funding to maintain your values, proving they are not easily compromised.

  You, as the founder, should have a clear idea of the Value Proposition as you are starting out. It will help you to attract not only donors, but great board members and other supporters. It can be fleshed out further by the board as you continue to grow, and it should focus on building trust with your donors[11].

- As a leader, you need to **be a mentor AND a mentee** for life. No one can be smart enough or experienced enough to know all of the answers you will need to know, so do not be afraid to surround yourself with other intelligent leaders you can learn from and who are not afraid to tell you when you are wrong. Being surrounded by all "yes men" is a dangerous place to be. Don't forget to pay it forward and mentor others on their way up!

---

[11] ("Nonprofit Value Proposition: 4 Proven Ways to Help Donors Understand Why They Should Give" by Nathan Hill) (reprinted with permission from NextAfter) NextAfter https://www.nextafter.com/blog/nonprofit-value-proposition-4-proven-ways-to-help-donors-understand-why-they-should-give/

# CHAPTER 5

# TAKING CARE OF BUSINESS

————— ••◉•• —————

*"You are only as good as your ability to pick and
keep good people."*

Paul Calistro
(Executive Director at West End
Neighborhood House)

## Board Formation

You will have started to form a board before applying for incorporation and nonprofit status. While the paperwork is being prepared and you are waiting for the official status, continue to recruit to round out your board. It will be tempting to surround yourself with your closest allies because they believe in you and probably have a lot of the same beliefs and desires, so they will be your first supporters. If these people are also passionate about the cause, and you believe they will be a big help, bring them on board (no pun intended!).

Your board will most likely change and evolve over time, so, for now, form the board needed to get the organization up and running. Then have the board re-evaluate itself and its needs in a year or two and adjust at that time. The structure and legal requirements of a nonprofit dictate that you, the founder, turn over the governance of the organization to the board. It may be a bit of a struggle between holding onto your original vision and letting it go to become the full-fledged organization you have created, but the turnover needs to happen as soon as the board is formed.

The founder may have a seat on the board, and may even serve as board chair[12], but the founder may only have one vote. The remaining directors also have one vote each. They should not just vote in a block to go along with the founder or another leader. Board members need to be willing and able to act in good faith and vote in the best interest of the organization and its mission.

Engaging the board early in ideas that you (the founder) are thinking about implementing can be key to the success of the new plan as well as the long-term success of the organization. The board should be made up of people you respect, who are talented, and who have great insight and varied experiences. Use their talents! They can help you think through the risks, questions you should ask if you will be going down the intended path, and what values should guide the work. In this early-stage consultation, you and the board should determine together what criteria to keep in mind as you design the new plan and if the plan makes sense.

If you go to the board after your plan is fully developed (even if it is only in your mind), it is unlikely you will be open to any push-back and may be looking for the board's stamp of approval. This could cause board members to feel under-valued and frustrated for being left out of the planning stages. It may create discord going forward.

The board is the over-arching governing body of a nonprofit. Its members have a responsibility to the organization as well as to the public to ensure all is being run properly and ethically and that they approach their work with integrity.

As the founder, it will be exciting to be surrounded by those who support you and the mission in these early days, but you also need to look ahead. Think about how you will feel years down the road with a highly engaged, empowered, independent governing body holding you and others accountable for advancing the mission.

From the beginning, the founder of the organization should have a **succession plan** – an exit strategy. This may be many years down the road, but the founder needs to be planning for the day when a new leader takes over. Many times, a strong founder will have a relatively weak board, meaning that the board members implicitly trust the founder to lead them. If you put together a board of only "yes men," rather than driving succession when the obvious time arrives, the board may continue to let you, the founder, lead because change can be uncomfortable.

---

[12] In this book "board chair" and "president" are used interchangeably. There are times when the founder becomes president, and there is a separate board chair. Other times, both roles may be filled by one person, or there may only be a president OR a chair.

It may be a good idea to find a mentor outside the organization who pledges to tell you when it is time for you to turn over the reins, as it may not be obvious to you and others within the organization.

## St. Francis Hospital

A local Wilmington, Delaware hospital was founded by the Sisters of Saint Francis of Philadelphia in 1924. The mission is to serve all who require expert medical care in the local area, regardless of religion, race, color, creed, or economic status.

In the late 1990s, the hospital had just formed the St. Francis Foundation to serve as its fundraising arm. The hospital CEO at that time recruited the CEO of a local construction company with extensive nonprofit board experience to run the Foundation board. He was a native Delawarean who knew a lot of community leaders, and he started by recruiting a few of them to join the board.

The hospital was serving a disproportionate share of the low-income patients in the area who were uninsured or underinsured, and, because of that, the hospital was losing money. The initial Foundation board members actively recruited other board members who had a passion for making sure the disadvantaged patients in Wilmington had access to great medical care, and who also had a broad reach in the community. Their passion was contagious, so they were able to recruit great board members who shared the vision and had access to potential funders.

Even though the hospital's finances were "in the red," it was doing some great things. The Foundation touted these successful programs in its advertising and fundraising. It shared that the  hospital had the best pre-natal care program in the state, defying the odds in all but eliminating the infant mortality rate, despite having some of the lowest-income patients. The hospital was also proud of having an aggressive program for the non-native-speaking immigrant population. The hospital took its mobile outreach van into high-risk areas, where the poorest members of the community congregated, to offer screenings and other medical care.

These successful programs were highlighted to start attracting funds. The need was so compelling, and the board members were so passionate, the money started to come in. Once the individual and corporate funding started flowing and the programs became more successful, the Foundation was able to qualify for grants and other funding sources. Then, it leveraged the early success and started to dream even bigger. In the first decade of the 2000s the Foundation raised more than $30 million and was able to help the hospital build a heart center, a bariatric center, and a new emergency room.

The hospital was not only able to continue serving its mission, but it was able to provide state-of-the-art healthcare to a community in desperate need. A passionate, well-connected, hard-working board was able to leverage the strengths of the organization and its board to enable the hospital to flourish.

You will need to find other people who are passionate about your nonprofit's mission, while also being able to broaden your scope. If your board is too insular (all family members or friends who are part of the same circles), you will have too narrow a scope to draw from for talent, expertise, and funding. Also, if you are planning to be a paid executive director from the start, your close associates may not want to fund your salary in lieu of funding the services you will be offering.

Each state requires a minimum number of directors, so check your requirements.[13] It is best to have a **minimum** of five (5) and a **maximum** of eighteen (18) directors on your board, with between eight (8) and fifteen (15) as the optimal sweet spot. If you have too few members, it will be hard to have enough attendees for a **quorum** (the minimum number of voting members of the Board of Directors required to be present in order to conduct business) for meetings and to get the important work done. If you have too many, it will be difficult to reach consensus to make the difficult decisions, and meetings will not be efficient in getting to the core of the work.

**The following are important considerations when recruiting new board members:**

- **Knowledge about and passion for the mission** is critical.
- **Diversity** – in age, race, gender (unless your organization is gender-specific), expertise, life experience, socio-economic status, and people with differing

---

[13] ("Nonprofit Board of Directors: Top 7 FAQs" [Updated January 2019]) Harbor Compliance https://www.harborcompliance.com/blog/2017/06/15/nonprofit-board-director-faq/

opinions will help make the organization more successful by offering broader points of view.

- One or two **visionaries with experience** who know how organizations are run and who know how to raise money can help steer the growth.

- **Politically active people** (but not those currently in office) and others with connections in the community will broaden your reach and visibility.

- If your organization's mission is to improve the lives of a vulnerable population, funders will be looking for you to have a few **community faces** on your board. They can educate the board and executive director on what is actually happening in the community to help them make better-informed decisions. These board members may also be "mission" board members who provide the "patient" or "community member" voice for those you are serving.

- A balance of "**thought leadership**" and "**worker bees**" is needed to get the organization up and running.

- Good **collaborators and strategizers** working together on the board will make the work easier to manage.

- People who are **willing to ask and face the hard questions** about the organization will challenge the status quo and bring about improvement.

- Board members must have **trust and respect for each other** so they are able to have the tough discussions on important issues, come to a consensus, and be able to continue to be collegial even when a vote does not go their way.

- Try to **avoid having only one token representative board member** from any given category or population segment. It can be very intimidating to that one person attempting to represent a whole sector. They may not feel empowered to speak up or provide the input the board should receive from them.

- A board member should understand all of the expectations and be willing to be "**all in**" before accepting the role.

**When forming the board, you may also consider:**

- Having a majority of your board members not related to each other or the founder/leader. If there is a vote on paying the founder's salary or other potential conflicts of interest, you want family members to be able to recuse[14]

---

[14] Recuse: to withdraw from the vote, and even the discussion leading up to the vote, so as not to sway opinions on the matter in which the person recusing has a conflict of interest

themselves from the vote while leaving a large enough board to still have a quorum.

- Having outsiders, rather than only those closest to you, can help to broaden your focus. You may find that you have been too close to the issues for too long, and you are not seeing the whole picture clearly.

- Adding one or two board members with nonprofit governance experience to help guide the organization through compliance requirements and best practices.

- Appointing board members with expertise your organization needs such as a CPA, attorney, banker, corporate sector employee, wealth manager, and/or healthcare experts. This will differ for each organization.

- If you add board members who will be able to write large checks, they may also be serving on four or five other boards for the same reason. Your organization will be the recipient of their donations, but you may only get a fraction of that person's energy for board duties.

- It may be tempting to try to recruit board members who have a lot of board experience, but try to ascertain whether or not they have capacity in their lives to give your board the attention needed. They may be spreading themselves too thin to be an effective board member.

- Structuring the board so there are "vice" or "assistant" positions that are understudies or backups to important officer roles like treasurer. The people in these roles can also be another layer of checks and balances when dividing up the duties. The assistant/vice chair of the committee or board could also be the next person in line for the role they are the backup for – the vice president knows they will become president, and the assistant treasurer will become the treasurer when the current member's term expires.

- Staggering the terms from the beginning by structuring A, B, and C groups. "A" members will be up for re-election after the first year, "B" members after two years, and "C" members after three years. This way not all board members are up for re-election in the same year. After the first re-election, each member would serve a full three-year term going forward.

- Overall term limits for directors. You may want to put a cap on how many two- or three-year terms an individual can serve before being required to take a break from board service.

- A minimum required "Give & Get" – how much board members are expected to individually donate (Give) or bring in from other sources (Get) – each year.
  - This could help ensure a steady stream of income each year.

○ Because grantors and other potential donors look at the percentage of board members who donate annually, you may consider requiring every member to donate each year. You could allow each director to decide how much they are comfortable giving (with no minimum requirement). Realize that this may still make some of the less financially stable board members uncomfortable because they know some people in the organization will see how little they donated.

○ It could be a financial barrier to entry for strong board candidates who do not have the financial means or community connections but may have precious knowledge about the community and those you are serving.

○ Other alternatives may be tiered levels of required giving to lessen the burden on younger or less affluent board members or a volunteer requirement in lieu of a cash donation. Some members will be willing and able to participate by service rather than by financial support.

○ Ultimately, you want a well-balanced board with a lot of expertise to further your mission. You do not want to lose great board members simply because they cannot afford steep donation requirements.

- You may also consider requiring volunteer time from all board members over and above the time spent on board meetings.

- Board members are volunteering their time, talent, and treasure, so the relationship will only work if they are passionate about the mission. Otherwise, it will begin to feel like a chore, and they may end up frustrated and not engaged.

- Try to employ the strengths of each board member so they will feel like they are contributing, that they are needed, and that they are making a difference.

- All board members need to understand their fiduciary duties and will need a clear understanding of the mission and what is expected of them.

Information about fiduciary duties and on-boarding training is in Chapter 6, and conflict of interest and board code of conduct policies will be discussed in Chapter 7.

When recruiting board members, be sure to ask for suggestions from your peer network and others you have met who are passionate about your mission. Depending on the type of organization you have, you may need fewer board members to carry out your mission. It is easier to add additional board seats as you grow rather than having to cut board seats later if you start with too many. The number one "skill" you want board members to have is passion for the mission. From there, you should look at the overall makeup of your board and consider what other skills, abilities, and reach your organization will need to have a diverse and well-rounded successful board.

The graphic above is an adaptation of Maslow's hierarchy of needs created by Chris Grundner, a nonprofit leader, to depict the building blocks and key ingredients that should go into building an exceptional board. [15] At the base, you have **passion** for the mission. It is a necessity, but passion alone will not get you to the apex of success or even help you reach long-term sustainability.

At the next level, you need to put in place **standards and best practices**. Board members must each understand their role and their **fiduciary duty** – their legal responsibility to the organization and the community. Nonprofit best practices need to be implemented such as term limits, annual reviews, rules that apply evenly to all members, job descriptions, and requiring that everyone in the organization is held accountable to follow the rules that have been implemented.

**Diversity** of skillsets, perspectives, and experience is necessary to elevate your board and your organization. Board meetings may be shorter with all like-minded

---

[15] ("Modern Nonprofit Board Governance – Passion is Not Enough!" by Chris Grundner [September 8, 2014]) TEDxWilmington YouTube https://www.youtube.com/watch?v=MIF9yJVldwQ

individuals at the table, but your nonprofit will reap a greater benefit with broader perspectives and members who challenge the status quo to prompt critical discussions. Perhaps most importantly, the perspective of the population you are serving should be adequately represented on the board.

There is dignity in serving on a board and in preserving the dignity of the individuals you are serving. Diversity on your board is crucial because there may be an unconscious bias of which you may not be aware if you do not have a mix of people all providing their input.

At the highest level of the pyramid is **Transcendent Leadership**, or looking past the leadership of today to ensure a long future. This requires planning for turnover to avoid temporary derailment when leaders leave with little warning, creating a pipeline of future board members who are groomed for future leadership, and mentoring current board members to prepare them for board officer roles.

As you add to your board or fill vacant board seats, first consider what expertise your board is lacking. Specifically strive to fill open positions with people who have the needed skills or connections. These needs will change as your organization changes, so, as seats become available, the board should re-evaluate what expertise is needed to round out the board.

## Becoming Official – Fiscal Year, Nonstock Charter, Incorporation, EIN, IRS Nonprofit Status, Logo, Domain Name, Etc.

The next steps you will take to set up your nonprofit will form the structure of your organization and will create a legal entity. Be very careful when filling out incorporation and IRS forms to give the correct information and to properly choose your intended status, or you may have a long journey to correcting it later. Consider using a professional to help you with the documents and forms.

1. Determine your **fiscal year dates**. Many organizations choose July 1-June 30 so they are not wrapping up "end-of-year" filings, financials, and other paperwork at the end of the calendar year when many nonprofits are concentrating on fundraising. Some do operate on a calendar year or other dates. Choose what makes sense for you. Think about when your busy season will be, and try to have a year-end that is not at the same time. You will use these dates when you incorporate and file for your 501(c)(3) status, as this will determine when your tax filings are due.

**Federal filings** are due on the fifteenth day of the fifth month following the organization's tax year-end date, so if your nonprofit's fiscal year ends on June 30, your federal 990 will be due on November 15. Depending on where you incorporate, the state will have requirements for annual filing of franchise or other taxes which may also be dependent on your fiscal year dates.

2. Some states require a short document called **Articles of Incorporation** or a **Certification of Formation**, but most require a **Nonstock Charter**, also known as a **Certificate of Incorporation**. A nonprofit has a "nonstock" charter because there is no stock issued and no dividends or income may be distributed to directors, officers, or individual members except as reasonable compensation for services rendered. The charter or certificate is the official document that states the name of the corporation, its registered address, its purpose, how it may operate, details about the board (terms, number of members, etc.), details about what must be included in the bylaws and how they may be amended, and what happens if the organization is dissolved. For an organization to qualify for exemption with the IRS, there are certain provisions that must be included in the organizing documents, so consult IRS.gov to be sure your documents are in compliance.[16] The charter or certificate is signed by an authorized officer, most likely the founder, and is filed with the state when incorporating.

3. Become **incorporated** by filing in the state of your choice. The majority of nonprofit organizations are corporations. In a few cases, nonprofits will incorporate as an LLC, but this usually only happens when existing nonprofit corporations want to join together as one tax-exempt nonprofit. There may be laws in your state against a 501(c)(3) organization being an LLC, and the IRS may not grant 501(c)(3) status to an LLC. Be sure to check into this further if you were considering an LLC nonprofit.

Applying for corporate status can be completed quickly, but for many organizations it can take a few weeks or months to complete. Start as soon as you have the name, charter, and physical address (not a post office box) for your organization or the registered agent's name and address. File the paperwork and pay the state fee for incorporation. In most cases, this can all be done online.

---

[16] ("Charity – Required Provisions for Organizing Documents" [Reviewed or Updated June 15, 2022]) IRS.gov https://www.irs.gov/charities-non-profits/charitable-organizations/charity-required-provisions-for-organizing-documents

A **registered agent** is a person or organization you appoint to be your statutory agent to receive legal notices, tax documents, and other government notices on behalf of your organization. There are a few reasons you may want to pay to hire a registered agent. First, if you do not yet have a brick-and-mortar location for your nonprofit, or if you expect to change addresses a few times, the registered agent can provide a permanent physical address for you. Their fee may also cover the federal and state filings due each year and can help you stay in compliance. Additionally, they can safely hold your corporate documents. Hiring a registered agent does come with a price, so you need to weigh your options carefully.

4. Apply for an **EIN**. Every corporation needs to have an Employer Identification Number (like a Social Security Number, but for a business) that is assigned by the IRS, even if it has no employees. When you apply online at https://sa.www4.irs.gov/modiein/individual/index.jsp, you receive the number almost instantly. File as a corporation that started a new business. The president, CEO, or other corporate officer will need to use their name and Social Security Number to apply. You will need the EIN number to apply for your 501(c)(3) status.

5. Apply for **501(c)(3) status** with the IRS. First, look at the IRS' list of things to do before filing.[17] To file, you will complete a Form 1023-series application and pay the application fee online at IRS.gov. Go to https://www.irs.gov/instructions/i1023ez to see if your organization will qualify to file the Form 1023-EZ rather than the larger Form 1023. The 1023-EZ is a much shorter form, and it will take less time to obtain your 501(c)(3) status if you qualify to file the EZ form. To determine your qualification, you will need to fill out a 30-question worksheet. (Most of the page in the IRS link above contains the instructions for how to answer the questions, and the worksheet itself can be found by scrolling all the way to the end.) If you answer "yes" to any one question, you are not eligible for the EZ form and must apply using Form 1023.

If your gross receipts (total income) are less than $50,000 per year for the first three years, you will also qualify to file the 990-N (e-postcard) tax return each year instead of the very cumbersome 990 form. There is an intermediary form, the 990-EZ Short Form Return, for an organization that

---

[17] ("Before Applying for Tax-Exempt Status" [Reviewed or Updated December 1, 2022]) IRS.gov https://www.irs.gov/charities-non-profits/before-applying-for-tax-exempt-status

has gross receipts less than $200,000 and total assets at the end of the tax year less than $500,000. Check with the IRS to see which is the right fit.

Depending on the type of form you file, it could take months to obtain certification of nonprofit status from the IRS. The good news is that once you do receive the notice, the tax-deductible status, to the full extent of the law, is retroactively applicable for your donors from the date you initially applied.

If you want donations to be tax-deductible for donors right away – if maybe your tax-exempt status will not be active until the next calendar year – you may consider starting your nonprofit under the umbrella of a community foundation or other existing nonprofit, but they may charge a fee for this service. If you plan to be a stand-alone nonprofit ultimately, and you are able to wait for the IRS certification, that is the preferable (and less expensive) option.

6. Create a **logo** for your organization that can be used on all outward-facing communications. If you are creative, you may do it, but know there are specific sizes and file types that printers and web designers will need. If you do not have access to creative software, you may want to hire a graphic artist or barter with them to create a logo in exchange for sponsorship or other advertisement at your events or on your website.

You can also consider a crowdsourcing site like crowdspring[18] where many graphic designers bid to create a logo that matches your specifications. This is a relatively inexpensive option to find a great design. I did this for a nonprofit organization about 10 years ago. They still use the logo, and it is instantly recognizable when people see it.

When designing a logo, think about the colors you would like to use that will be associated with your brand going forward. Try to choose colors that are traditional and not just trending at the moment. Think about the ease of duplicating your colors for branded items (promotional merchandise) you may use. Also consider how the logo will look in black and white when you do not have the option to print in color.

The logo should mesh with your mission. Use fonts that are easy to read. There are far too many "fancy" logos where it is impossible to figure out the name of the organization! This defeats the purpose of a logo, which is to make your organization's brand easily recognizable and understood.

---

[18] There are many other crowdsource options, and I only list crowdspring because I had personal experience with them in 2012. Be sure to research your options and get references to find a legitimate source.

Think about whether to use graphics in your logo. You need the logo to be as easy to understand and recognize on a large banner as it is on a small brochure, so consider how the type and graphics will look in different sizes, shapes, and formats. Determine whether the graphic will be easy to reproduce and how it may look if it is reproduced using a low-quality printer or copier. On some social media pages or in ads, there may be a size and shape requirement, so consider how the logo will look in square, round, oval, or rectangular spaces. Is there a way to fit only a piece of it and still remain recognizable?

It may work well for you to put together a small focus group to give feedback on logo options before you settle on one. Including marketing/branding experts as well as non-experts (everyday folks) will give you different perspectives you may not have considered. They should focus on readability, how it relates to your mission, and even how it may look like something other than what you anticipated or were able to see on your own. Of course, you may pick and choose which suggested changes you adopt, then go back to the designer to make revisions.

Your logo may change over time as your organization evolves, but **you want a logo and brand that people recognize, know, and trust that serves your nonprofit well for a long time**. Rebranding can be expensive and time consuming because it means changing all printed materials, your website and social media channels, signage, etc.

7. If your **family** is involved with the nonprofit, be sure to put up boundaries. First, you do not want even an appearance of impropriety or favoritism of a family member over another board or staff member. This may have begun as a "family business," but it quickly needs to become something broader to be able to stand on its own. This means deferring to the board you have selected to make the decisions as a group, with the board passing those decisions to the staff or volunteers to carry out.

Additionally, you want to put up boundaries within your family, so this organization does not become all-encompassing in your life. Consider creating "safe zones" or "safe times" where the nonprofit is not discussed. There is a time for the organization, and a separate non-organization time for friends and family. Depending on why you started the nonprofit, there can be a lot of emotion involved in it, and you do not want this to define your relationships outside the organization.

8. Make a **succession plan** to extricate yourself (the founder) from the organization down the road. You are passionate about the organization, you

are the reason all of these people are involved and immersed in the cause, but you need to plan for the next level for the organization's sake. There is more about succession planning in Chapters 6 and 10.

9. In doing your research before starting the charity, you have most likely found organizations in other locations that are doing similar work. **Model your organization after what has worked** for them and improve upon that model. There is no need to re-invent the wheel. You can move ahead and be successful twice as fast if you use the hard work and research that has already been done by others, find where they may still be lacking, and put it together to make a new and improved service to others, while not duplicating existing efforts in your area.

10. Buy the **domain name** that you will want to use for your website as early as possible, so you will own it when you are ready to set up your online presence. There are sharks out there who snatch up possible names for organizations, and then they profit by selling that name for a much higher price to the organization that is desperate to own the name.

Domain names ending in .org are most popular for nonprofits and lend the most credibility, but there are many other options like .net, .com, .info, and at least a dozen other choices. Choose the first half of your name (the part before the "dot," i.e., "bestnonprofit"), then look at GoDaddy.com[19] to see how much it would cost to purchase the domain for that name with the different ending options (bestnonprofit.org, bestnonprofit.net, bestnonprofit.info, etc.). Be sure to consider which ending people will most likely search for if they are trying to find your website.

11. Develop an **ethical culture** from the start. Ethics and transparency will be covered in more depth in different chapters of this book. To start, you may want to look at the American Society of Public Administration's code of ethics[20] to follow their guide to best practices.

Some boards create a Code of Ethics document so the expectations of board members are clear. The board must then self-govern to hold itself and its members accountable.

---

[19] The domain may be purchased from other domain vendors, but GoDaddy makes it easy to check the availability of domain names, looking at different variations of the name.
[20] ("Code of Ethics" [2022]) ASPA.org
https://www.aspanet.org/ASPA/ASPA/Code-of-Ethics/Code-of-Ethics.aspx

# CHAPTER 6

# BOARD'S FIRST STEPS

⸻ • ● • ⸻

*"For something to grow, it must be planted
on good ground."*

Brother Ronald Giannone
(Founder of Ministry of Caring)

### Sean's House

In July 2018 the Locke family lost their beloved son and brother to suicide. Sean had been a great athlete in high school and college. He was well liked, and he had many close friends. After he graduated from college, Sean landed a good job and all seemed to be well. Unfortunately, no one knew that Sean, the outwardly happy, active, friendly guy, was also suffering alone with depression. The loss caught all of his friends and family members off guard.

After this tragedy, the family, with the help of their friends, started SL24: Unlocke the Light Foundation (named after Sean and his #24 basketball jersey number) in December 2018. The aim was to get young people talking about their depression and suicidal thoughts, often brought on following trauma, as the first step in getting them help before it is too late.

There was not a program like this in the area. Sean's dad started speaking to audiences at local high schools and colleges, and before long he was being asked to share their family's painful story all over the state. He spoke to young people, their friends and family members, and even Airmen at the Dover Air Force Base to help them recognize the signs of suicidal thoughts and depression, and to teach them how to get help to prevent future tragedies.

The Locke family put together a diverse board.[21] Its members all had a passion for the cause. They were diverse in background, gender, age, and race, and many had long-standing connections and reach in the broader community.

Early on, the board decided the next step for the organization was to open Sean's House, a house near the college campus where Sean and his roommates had lived during college. The house would be a physical location where young people in the fourteen to twenty-four age range could go for peer counseling or just to have a safe space to go when they needed to take a breath. Donations and offers to hold fundraisers to support the renovation of the house and the operations poured in because people in the community saw the need for mental health support, especially for young people. The board members and the family's friends were eager to help prevent this tragedy from happening in another family. Sean's House held its grand opening in October 2020.

In its first four years, SL24: Unlocke the Light Foundation has raised over $1 million and has trained 156 volunteer peer counselors (Peer24) to work with visitors to the house. Events such as therapeutic dog visits, student-athlete dinners, and fraternity and sorority cookouts have drawn students in and made them feel comfortable in the house. Some visit for a free cup of coffee or a cookie, to sit at the dining room table to do homework, or to borrow a book from the extensive library. Some of the visitors seek out peer counseling. Around 17,000 visitors have come to Sean's House in the two years that the house has been open, with more than 4,000 Peer24 Support sessions conducted and 87 people saved from a crisis situation.[22]

SL24: Unlocke the Light Foundation and Sean's House will be successful long into the future because it started slowly but passionately with focus on the mission. The organization raised the funds needed to renovate and operate Sean's House before starting the work, is holding reserves for future operating costs, and has a committed and diverse board that knows its fiduciary duty to the organization. The organization has successfully transitioned to adding paid staff members who are also passionate about the mission.

---

[21] Full disclosure: I have been a board member since 2019.

[22] Statistics on SL24: Unlocke the Light Foundation and Sean's House as of December 2022

SL24 is a shining example of how having a mission that others will get behind and bringing together a diverse group of people who have passion for the mission but also experience and reach in the community will create a successful nonprofit.

Almost all nonprofit board members are unpaid volunteers.[23] They have three primary legal duties known as the duty of care, duty of loyalty, and duty of obedience.[24]

1. Duty of Care: Take care of the nonprofit by ensuring prudent use of all assets, including facilities, people, and goodwill.

2. Duty of Loyalty: Ensure the nonprofit's activities and transactions are, first and foremost, advancing its mission; Recognize and disclose conflicts of interest; Make decisions that are in the best interest of the nonprofit corporation, not in the best interest of the individual board member (or any other individual or for-profit entity).

3. Duty of Obedience: Ensure the nonprofit obeys applicable laws and regulations, follows its own bylaws, and that the nonprofit adheres to its stated corporate purposes/mission.

Some would say the fourth primary legal duty is Transparency. Transparency, in the nonprofit sense, is defined as the widespread availability of relevant, reliable information about the performance, financial position, and governance of the organization.[25] Governance is "the act or process of governing or overseeing the control and direction of something (such as a country or an organization)."[26] Board members also provide guidance by contributing to the organization's culture, strategic focus, effectiveness, and financial sustainability, as well as serving as ambassadors and advocates of the organization.

Directors should always strive to put the organization above their personal interests and be transparent and ethical in all votes, actions, and financial responsibilities. Volunteer directors may be protected from liability in running the organization, but

---

[23] ("Can Board Members Be Paid?" [2022]) National Council of Nonprofits Nonprofits (Reprinted with permission from the National Council of Nonprofits.) https://www.councilofnonprofits.org/tools-resources/can-board-members-be-paid

[24] ("Board Roles and Responsibilities" [2022]) National Council of Nonprofits Nonprofits (Reprinted with permission from the National Council of Nonprofits.) https://www.councilofnonprofits.org/tools-resources/board-roles-and-responsibilities

[25] ("Transparency in Non-Profit Organizations" [April 28, 2017]) BKC Certified Public Accountants, PC https://www.bkc-cpa.com/transparency-in-non-profit-organizations/

[26] https://www.merriam-webster.com/dictionary/governance

only if there is found to be no grossly negligent conduct. Your organization should add the protection of **Directors and Officers (D & O) Insurance** which protects those individuals from personal losses if they are sued over actions they took while serving as a director or officer.

After the initial board is chosen by the founder, one of the main responsibilities of the board should be development of and recruitment for future board seats. Care should be taken to have a "people pipeline" or "leadership pipeline" where potential future board members learn about the organization by volunteering on committees and getting involved in other capacities. Consider having "vice" or "assistant" board roles (e.g., assistant treasurer, vice chair) where you are developing future leaders who will move up to the role they are assisting after a term or two, or co-chairs for certain committees to divide the work. This way there are members who can fill in if a board or committee member is absent or suddenly not able to fulfill their duties.

Once the board is formed, it is that entity that is charged with running the organization. The board members need to ensure the nonprofit is being run correctly and is mission-focused. If the board determines the best course of action for the good of the mission is to replace the founder/leader, they must act on that decision.

## Board Training

Invite prospective board members to attend a board meeting so they can ask questions about the organization and how it is run. Hold a meet and greet so prospective members can meet those already on the board and get to know them.

Before a board member attends a meeting for the first time, each member should go through **on-boarding and training**. They should understand the story of the organization, its mission, and the way the board meetings will operate. Each member should fill out the Conflict-of-Interest Policy and should read and sign a copy of the Whistleblower Policy and any other organizational policies. (See Chapter 7 for a list of policies you may choose to develop.) Each new member should be provided with a copy of the bylaws, organizational chart, a calendar of events for the next fiscal year, and a board roster with names and contact information for all board members.

## Meetings & Minutes

**At the inaugural meeting of the board of directors, the formalities of the organization's structure and governance should be voted on and adopted.** This would include creating and adopting bylaws, adopting mission and vision statements, and electing officers. Be sure that if the bylaws require a supermajority to change them, a supermajority votes the bylaws into being. (See more about the bylaws and supermajority votes later in this chapter.)

The board should formally **accept the mission and vision statements** of the organization. If the founder created the mission and vision statements before the board was formed, the board may want to do some wordsmithing to be sure the mission and vision accurately represent the organization's intentions. Once the board agrees the mission and vision statements are worthy declarations, they should put them to an official vote.

Be sure to record the **meeting minutes**, beginning with the board's first meeting. If a secretary has not yet been elected, ask for a volunteer to accurately record the discussions that take place. The minutes are the written record of the discussions, decisions, and votes that take place in a meeting. They need to record the final actions decided upon with enough of the discussion details to ensure that the board has done its due diligence, but the record does not need to include every small detail in the discussion. The secretary will need to use some discretion as to what is included, and the other board members can help determine the level of detail required.

The minutes are the official record of your organization, so it is very important to record all activity, including financial records. Your bylaws will spell out which items require a board vote, and the minutes will provide the name of the person who made the motion to be voted on, which board member seconded, and the final vote tally – for, against, and abstentions. **The minutes for all meetings should be stored in a central location and safely kept for the life of the organization.**

The minutes should be discussed and approved by a board vote at the following meeting to ensure that the record accurately reflects the discussions, decisions, and votes that took place. It is helpful to type up and send the minutes to the board members to review within a week of the meeting recorded, when there is still memory of the discussion and details, so the record may be adjusted if corrections need to be made.

The bank may require a copy of the minutes that show the authorization of new members when they are to be added as signers on the account. Minutes should also be submitted to the accounting firm as part of audit records when an audit is being performed.

At every meeting, the board secretary should also record the attendance to establish a quorum and to track board member participation. If the bylaws or other directives require a minimum board meeting attendance number or percentage, the president should consult with the secretary regularly, and should speak to those members who are approaching the number of missed meetings that require action. It may be decided that those members need to step down from their board positions, and new members should be appointed. Sometimes it is due to illness or other life circumstances, so try to keep the good board members involved in some other way. You may consider re-nominating them to the board in the future when they have the time to devote again.

Board meetings should be held at regular intervals. The recommended minimum number of meetings per year is four. I have found that board members tend to lose momentum and passion for the projects they are working on "offline" (outside of the meetings) after a few weeks, so it works best to meet every month or so to reignite the passion. I have been a part of boards that meet every other month or quarterly, and it seems that a lot is accomplished immediately following each meeting, but then it wanes after a few weeks until the next meeting. Board members have busy lives, and they, like most of us, put out the fire in front of them at the moment, and put everything else on the back burner.

It is best to set the meeting dates for the coming fiscal year and announce them. That way all directors can plan to attend. Consider whether you will provide the technology for virtual as well as in-person attendance.

If you have an Advisory Council, you may want to extend an invitation to them to attend the board meetings, too, so they can be reminded of all the good work you are doing and can provide input in their field of expertise. Be sure to give them the meeting dates well in advance and remind them as the time approaches.

## Financial Literacy

All board members need to understand their fiduciary duty in serving on a nonprofit board. It is imperative that each member learns how to read and understand financial statements and requires access to the financials at each meeting, or at least on a quarterly basis. If certain expenses are significantly over budget or look questionable for any reason, it is the board's duty to look into the details to ensure that the funds are being well managed. Training to understand the profit and loss statements (and to question them) should be part of the on-boarding process to ensure that those board members without previous business experience are on a level playing field with those who have a business background.

## Paid Staff vs. Volunteers

Determine if the founder will be a paid leader from the start. The board should consult with members of peer networks and other similar organizations to get outside opinions on this. Remember, the public and potential funders will be looking at what percentage of your funding goes directly to the cause you wish to serve. The overhead, including salaries and payroll taxes not directly attributable to programs, are not considered part of the money going directly to your mission. A good aim is for overhead expenses (management/general and fundraising expenses that support the organization but do not go directly to those you serve) to remain below 25% of the total expenses for most nonprofit structures. If salaries (not part of program expenses), taxes, and other overhead expenses are $50,000, you should be spending at least $150,000 on direct programming.

The 20-25% rule varies depending on the type of nonprofit organization. If your organization charges fees to attend shows (like art or dance), you may need to spend up to 35% on overhead to attract the maximum number of attendees.[27]

## Bylaws

**One of the first and most important acts for the board is to create and officially adopt bylaws.[28] The bylaws will be the backbone of the organization. They are an extension of the charter/certificate of incorporation that spells out the number of board members and other details about the organization, but the bylaws will be much more detailed. You may find sample bylaws (from similar organizations or online) to use as a guide, but it is best to find an attorney with nonprofit experience to prepare them.**

The bylaws should apply to all members of the organization, whether staff, board members, or volunteers. They should not be amended to fit a particular case or loophole. There are always temptations to find a way to keep a valuable person on the board when the bylaws clearly spell out term limits, or to hire someone's relative if the bylaws forbid it, but this is a slippery slope. The bylaws were crafted in the best interest of the organization, and careful consideration should be taken anytime amendments are made.

---

[27] ("Nonprofits May Need to Spend a Third of Their Budget on Overhead to Thrive – Contradicting a Donor Rule of Thumb" by Hala Altamimi & Qiaozhen Liu [September 22, 2022]) The Chronicle of Philanthropy https://www.philanthropy.com/article/nonprofits-may-need-to-spend-a-third-of-their-budget-on-overhead-to-thrive-contradicting-a-donor-rule-of-thumb

[28] See sample bylaws at 501Guide.com

The board is charged with strictly adhering to the organization's mission and to following the bylaws to the letter. If some bylaws become outdated or stop making sense for the day-to-day operations, the bylaws will spell out what is needed for the board to amend them. The board should make a practice of reviewing the bylaws every year or two to be sure they are being followed and that they still make sense. **Best practices maintain that a 2/3 board vote be required to amend the bylaws.**

**Term limits** for officers and board members are very important. If members are allowed to serve for an indefinite amount of time, there becomes a sort of "group think" that is hard for any new board members to break through. New ideas are discouraged, and the organization may not have the opportunity to grow when times and circumstances change.

Consider having a one-year "trial" on the board for each new member, and then, if they prove to be a good board member, they may serve two or three consecutive three-year terms (a maximum cap of nine or ten years). After serving the maximum years/terms, even if they are a valuable member, require a one-year wait to be considered for a new term.

Officers (president, vice presidents, secretary, treasurer, and any others you designate) have more intense roles, so they could serve one or two two-year terms in the executive committee role, but then be allowed to cycle to a different board role to finish out their total of nine or ten years. Because directors may cycle in and out of officer roles that have different term limits, the maximum cap is not always going to fit nicely into the "three terms times three years" format. The governance chair or other designated board member should keep track of each member's dates – when the current term ends, how many terms they have served, and the overall "expiration date" when they are required to roll off the board.

The bylaws should clearly spell out the roles of officer and non-officer board members and the number and frequency of board meetings. They should define what constitutes a quorum (the minimum number of voting members of the Board of Directors required to be present in order to conduct business). It is also important to specify the types of votes requiring a majority to carry a motion vs. the types of votes (like changing the bylaws) that will require a 2/3 vote (or other defined supermajority).

You may want to have **meeting attendance requirements** for board members. It may make sense to require directors to attend a minimum of 2/3 of the regular meetings to remain in good standing. It should also be made clear (in the bylaws or the Trustee Letter of Commitment) what the consequences will be if they are unable to fulfill their obligations.

Institute a succession plan for board resignations and vacancies, and have the outline of a plan for the removal of a board member. Spell out what could trigger an automatic removal, and add some broader language to consider some other scenarios that will lead to consideration for removal, who needs to vote on it, and how it will be handled.

When creating the bylaws, take the long view. Create them thinking of the future and what the organization may encounter, and try to make the bylaws stand the test of time. However, they will be flexible and amendable if and when change is needed.

## Mission & Vision Statements

Mission and vision statements are usually mentioned as connected thoughts. While they are both necessary, each has its own purpose. A lot of thought, discussion, and wordsmithing should go into both. They must be clearly defined and broad enough to be flexible for the future (don't box yourself in), but narrow enough to mean something (do not plan to be everything to everyone). The mission and vision statements are the backbone of all that your organization will do. Even so, know that if your nonprofit outgrows its initial mission and vision statements at some point, you can always revise them later.

A Mission Statement is the pronouncement of what your organization's focus is today and every day. This is what will drive your board, staff, and volunteers and keep them on the same path, heading in the same direction. Your Statement should be succinct and to the point, while being very clear as to your intent. It should be narrow enough to give your organization focus and purpose, but broad enough to allow for growth. This Statement will steer you in tough times or through times when you start to veer off course.

Be flexible with the Mission Statement intent and meaning as you grow, but be very careful not to let others coax you into stretching your mission to be something you never intended. This "mission creep" can happen when certain funders tempt you with promised donations that are tied to doing work outside your original scope. The board must be prepared to stick to the mission even as outsiders may try to steer the program off course or try to expand the mission with offers of funding for things not quite "on mission."

The Vision Statement is your organization's hope for the future. It is the "pie-in-the-sky idea" of what could be if your nonprofit is successful and does its job correctly.

It could be something like "Our vision is to eliminate hunger in our country." This is a lofty goal, but one you are striving toward. The Vision needs to be specifically related to your organization, and not just a general "we want everyone to be happy" sentiment.

While you put a lot of thought into the mission and vision statements, also consider what you envision for the work of the nonprofit. Are you imagining this as a perpetual nonprofit, or is it something you believe will accomplish most of its work in the next few years (or the next decade)? Do you aim to keep it small, or do you have grand plans for a much larger organization? You can always adjust at a future point, but it is good for all to be on the same page as to what you are working toward.

## A Nonprofit IS a Business

There is a myth that running a nonprofit is easier than running a business because it is made up of mostly volunteers and staff members who are usually paid less than in the corporate world. Nothing could be further from the truth! In fact, in many ways, running a nonprofit is more difficult because of those factors.

A nonprofit is a business. It is a corporation, and while its aim isn't to make a profit, it does need to have a business plan, has a need to raise money to run its programs, and the organization needs to be competitive in the marketplace. There needs to be an infrastructure with a workflow chart, policies and procedures for all to follow, and logistics plans. Additionally, there are sustainability and scalability concerns.

## Business License

Check with your local municipality and state licensing offices to see if a business license is required. In Delaware, nonprofit corporations are required to register with the Division of Revenue, to withhold Delaware State income taxes for any employees performing services within the state, and to register with the Delaware Department of Labor. In Florida, you need to file with the Department of Agriculture to register for your Solicitation of Contributions and renew it annually, but the state does not require you to have a business license. You will want to check in your state to see what filings they require.

## Human Resources

Once a nonprofit has employees, there will be human resources (HR) considerations and policies, and this could possibly require the addition of office space and other overhead. In hiring for a nonprofit, look for people who are not only passionate about the mission, but who are also good business people.

## Strategic Plan

Your nonprofit needs a strategic plan to advance its mission in the long run. "It ensures that everyone, from your board to your leadership to your staff, is on the same page about your nonprofit's mission, vision, values, and most important priorities."[29]

Every few years your board and staff members should go through a strategic planning process to look at where you want to be in three to five years, and then create a bridge of steps and procedures to get there. First, you will take a look at your mission and vision statements to be sure they still aptly fit your goals and whether or not you have been sticking to those goals. Then you do "big" thinking about where you want to be a few years down the road, and go through the steps to connect the dots from today to that point. This process may develop new committees and programs to work toward the specific goals.

It is best to go through the strategic process with an experienced outside facilitator who can help avoid your trigger points and to mediate any strong discussions or disagreements. Nonprofit support organizations will be able to connect you to people who specialize in this process.

## Bank Account

Once all of your paperwork is filled out, filed, and you have received approval as an official corporation with 501(c)(3) status, you will need to open a bank account. You cannot open a nonprofit bank account until you are "official," so as soon as you are, this should be the next priority. (Before that time, you could open a separate bank account that would not qualify for nonprofit perks, or you could talk to a local community foundation about opening a temporary account under their nonprofit umbrella if you already have donations coming in.) It is never okay to use a personal bank account for your nonprofit. You do not want even the appearance that your personal funds are mixing with the organization's funds.

Do research with banks in your local area to learn about fees they charge a nonprofit (try to avoid fees, if possible) and what they require to open an account. Most, if not all, will require your Articles of Incorporation or Nonstock Charter signed by an officer of the corporation, board meeting minutes that reflect the votes accepting the Charter, proof of incorporation with the state, proof of IRS nonprofit status, and a

---

[29] ("A Nonprofit Strategic Plan Example to Inspire Your Organization" by Lindsay Mullen [July 21, 2020]) Prosper Strategies https://prosper-strategies.com/nonprofit-strategic-plan-example/

list of the current board members. All who will be signers on the account will need to fill out signature cards. Open a simple checking account to start, so you can begin to accept donations.

Determine at your first board meeting how many signers you will have. It is recommended that you have at least three unrelated authorized signers and require two of them to sign every check. It can be a long, difficult process to change the authorized signers, so be sure to wisely choose people who are trustworthy, are in the local area to be available to sign, and who you expect to be on the board for a number of years.

Most banking and bill paying is done online these days, so carefully determine who has access to the online bank account and who has authorization to send out checks through the account. What is the procedure to receive that authorization?

If you are using a DBA name different from your corporate name, you will need to file separate paperwork with the state and then with the bank to be able to accept checks written to that name. Be sure to check with your bank for their requirements.

## Use of Software

As soon as possible, look into moving from keeping all of your records hand-written or on multiple spreadsheets to using software that can be saved in the cloud. This can help keep you organized, keep your documents safe and accessible, and will make running reports much easier. See Chapter 11 for more suggestions and details.

# CHAPTER 7

# DAY-TO-DAY BEST PRACTICES

————— ·•●•· —————

*"At the end of the day, integrity wins."*

Sharece Sellem-Hannah
(Playwright, Director)

The board and staff members of a nonprofit are constantly balancing the day-to-day work with the need to plan for the future. There is also a lot of juggling between the operations management and the work to fulfill the mission. Successful nonprofits are mission-based and constituency-driven, so your daily work should be focused with this in mind.

## Board Meetings

The board chair should consult with the board secretary and the executive director to create a **meeting agenda** prior to each meeting. It should list all topics that will be covered along with the name of the person(s) who will be leading the discussion on each topic. It is helpful to include a time limit for each topic on the agenda, so you can try to stick to an overall timeline.

A meeting packet that includes the agenda, committee reports from each chair, a treasurer's financial report, and other supporting documents for the meeting should be emailed to the directors and other meeting attendees ahead of the meeting. Every attempt should be made to distribute the packets at least a week before the scheduled meeting, so all will have a chance to look over the materials.

Many times, there is a lot to cover during a board meeting, so requiring the members to read the materials prior to the meeting can save a lot of time. They should come prepared to ask questions and vote on issues. If you have to go through each committee report line by line, it will make the meetings long and cumbersome, and it will eat into the time needed for discussion and decision making.

Board meetings need to be run in accordance with your written bylaws. This includes the timing of scheduled meetings (quarterly, every other month, monthly) and the amount of notice (a week, 10 days, two weeks, or a month prior) that is given to the board ahead of regularly-scheduled and special board meetings.

The number (or percentage of the total) of board members needed for a quorum should be specified in the bylaws. At the first board meeting where a quorum is present, the board should vote to adopt the bylaws, other governing documents, and elect board officers.

When each board meeting starts, the board chair should establish that there is a quorum present so any votes taken during the meeting will be valid. The chair should also confirm that the secretary (or other member) is there to record the minutes of the meeting as well as board member attendance.

The board should start the meeting by discussing the prior meeting minutes, ask and answer any questions, note any corrections, then vote the minutes (with corrections) into the permanent record. Next, go through all agenda items, leaving time for any new business at the end of the meeting. The body of the meeting should focus on mission-based business, current activities, and programs. Then the "New Business" open forum at the end can bring up new ideas that may be outside the scope of current or previous programming.

It is best to develop a culture of learning and innovation in your organization. All new ideas should be welcomed and considered. New board members should feel comfortable suggesting a new way of doing something, even if older or longer-term board members "tried it in 1992, and it didn't work." Times, circumstances, and the world around us change constantly, so a "new old" idea may just work today.

It may be a good idea to occasionally have a time during meetings for **"quantity over quality"** where all ideas, no matter how far-out they may be or whether they were tried previously, are thrown out there, and are welcomed and considered. Give all ideas a shot, and you may find a novel solution to that nagging problem.

If the discussion for any agenda item is running over its time limit, consider assigning a person or committee to look further into the topic to bring back to the full board at the next meeting, asking the few members who are "getting into the weeds" if they can discuss it among themselves after the meeting ("off line"), or consider tabling the topic for further discussion at the next board meeting.

If new ideas are presented or there are problems that need to be explored further, **special committees** may be formed according to the bylaws. (One board I served on called these "pop-up committees.") This way the discussion at the time-limited board meeting can be shelved, and the committee can bring its findings to present to the whole board at a future board meeting.

An **Executive Session** should be included at the end of every meeting once the organization has paid employees. This is a time when the staff members are excused and the board takes time to privately discuss the executive director or staffing issues, compensation, or other sensitive and confidential issues. If you only call an Executive Session when there is a problem, it may worry the staff members when they are excused. It is also better to discuss any small problems as they arise. This way, they may be addressed before they turn into large problems or before there becomes a need to fire someone.

There may be times when there are problems that need to be addressed. The board is representing the organization and its constituents, and if they find cause to act, they have the responsibility to take that action.

## Unanimous Written Consent

Occasionally, a matter arises that cannot wait until the next board meeting for a vote. The board chair may wish to take a board vote via email. Most states that permit action by written consent require unanimous approval. Each member's email vote should be through "reply all," so all members see every vote. Once an action by written consent is agreed to by all of the directors, the written consent resolution will have the same effect as a unanimous vote at a meeting of the board.[30]

## Board Best Practices

- Some boards follow the **Robert's Rules of Order** method of running meetings, others have adapted those rules to make their meetings less formal, and the rest have created their own methods of running a meeting. Using Robert's Rules, the board first establishes that there is a quorum; then approves the agenda; and for items that will be voted on, a motion is made, then debated, amended as needed, then voted on (all in favor, all opposed, any abstaining).

---

[30] ("Voting by Unanimous Written Consent" [November 15, 2021]) CharityLawyer https://charitylawyerblog.com/2021/11/15/voting-by-unanimous-written-consent/

Robert's Rules were first created and used for parliamentary procedures over 100 years ago, so they are very formal, but they are meant to maintain order and fairness. It is important that the board members and board chair have a basic understanding of the use and purpose of Robert's Rules and adapt them to fit the organization.

- **Financial reports** should be updated and presented to board members at least quarterly. Board members have a fiduciary duty to ensure the organization is financially sound, so they need to understand the financial reports and know there are funds available when they vote on expenditures.

- The secretary and the board chair should be tracking board member meeting participation to be sure all members are engaged. Procedures should be in place to contact those board members who have missed too many meetings (according to the bylaws), making it clear the steps that should be taken. Ask board members directly if they are engaged with the organization, and suggest they move on if not.

- About halfway through the fiscal year, the board chair and the Nominating Committee should be looking at which members' terms expire at the end of the year and which roles need to be filled.

- **Items to be reviewed at the Annual Meeting:**
  - Each committee should present its goals for the next fiscal year, including programs, funding, and expenses.
  - **The directors should consider doing a self-assessment of the board and an annual review of the organization to continue to improve effectiveness. Look at strengths, weaknesses, opportunities, and threats (SWOT analysis) of the board and the whole organization.**
  - An annual organization budget should be discussed, with an official vote when agreed upon.
  - Introduce and elect new board members.

- **Annually or Biannually:**
  - The board meetings will be very full with the day-to-day details of running the organization, but consider having a special board retreat meeting once or twice a year that can take the focus from the daily to the future. You may want to hire a consultant to facilitate a strategic planning session to look three to five years out.
  - **Send a survey** to board members annually to assess how the board, paid leadership, and the organization are doing.

○ The board chair, with the Executive Committee (made up of the board chair, vice chair(s), treasurer, secretary, the governance chair, and any others stated in the bylaws), should look at all accounts the organization has where **user names and passwords** are required. Be aware of who has access to that private information, and who should be added, deleted, or updated.

Appoint a person or committee to maintain that information and make changes as needed. You should change the passwords on a regular basis, know who will change them, who needs to be informed of the changes, and where a permanent record of the current login information for the accounts will be kept. Consider a cloud-based password keeper that more than one person knows how to access.

## Governance

Governance is the most important work a nonprofit board of directors will engage in. There are many facets to proper governance including abiding by and enforcing the bylaws, and implementing and enforcing policies and procedures.

**Guidelines & Standards a nonprofit may want to adopt:**

1. **Governing Guidelines**
   ○ They list the mission, charitable purpose, membership information, board and executive committee makeup, roles of board members and officers, and other details.
   ○ These may be used as informal bylaws until bylaws can be crafted and adopted.

2. **Guidelines for Contracts and Expenses**
   ○ These are clear procedures listing who may enter into a contract on behalf of the organization and who is authorized to sign a contract.
   ○ Set expense limits over which amount the board will need to vote to approve the expenditure (if outside a committee's budget limit).

3. **Communications Standards**
   ○ This document should spell out the dos and don'ts for all organizational communications including media publications, social media posts, and links that refer back to your website or other online locations.
   ○ It should include information about what types of postings need to be pre-approved and by whom, what types of communications are included,

how your name and logo should appear (capital and lower-case letters in parts of your corporate name, color codes for colors used in logo, etc.), and any other details you want to remain consistent for branding purposes.

○ Spell out how artwork used in posts is to be prepared and in what format.

○ If you include statistics about your organization (how many years you have been operating, how many people served, dollars raised, etc.), make it clear who in the organization is charged with knowing and updating that information to supply it for publications.

○ Detail what types of information you do not want to have included in public communications.

○ List the positions/roles that are cleared to post to social media and what parameters those people are held to for posts (no personal viewpoints or self-promoting).

○ Clearly spell out what positions/roles are cleared to submit press releases and other outward-facing media submissions.

○ Be sure you know who has access to the passwords for social media accounts and who manages that access.

○ If someone in the organization needs a link prepared for an event or special sign-up, supply a form for them to fill out that gives all of the details needed for the event landing page. Know who in your organization will process these forms.

**Policy Documents that should be created by, agreed to, and signed off on by the board:**

1. **Conflict of Interest Policy**

○ A conflict of interest arises when an individual's personal (or a close family member's) interests could compromise their professional interests or duties.

○ Each director should fill out the form listing any potential conflicts with their family members, employers, personally owned businesses, or other interests, and these forms should be signed, dated, and turned in **annually.**

○ If a director knows that they will have a **conflict or potential conflict** with a particular item on the agenda, they should declare it at the outset of the board meeting and, if it is determined by the board to be an issue, that member should **recuse** themselves from all discussion and voting on that issue. They should not remain in the room for any consideration of that issue, so as not to taint the discussion or even create an appearance of having influence over the outcome.

## 2. Confidentiality Agreement

○ This agreement spells out to board members what organizational information is to remain private.

○ It is an especially good policy when you have a number of inexperienced board members, but it is a good reminder for those seasoned members, too.

○ This agreement should also be signed and dated by each board member, but **once during their term** is sufficient.

## 3. Code of Conduct Policy[31]

○ This policy may also be called a statement of values or code of ethics. It outlines the principles and standards your board members must follow.

○ This is a more comprehensive policy that can include the Conflict of Interest and Confidentiality Policies, mission and vision statements, as well as a list of fiduciary responsibilities to make them clear to all board members.

○ The organization may also have separate code of conduct policies for volunteers, employees, or other groups.

## 4. Whistleblower Policy

○ The Sarbanes-Oxley Act of 2002 (SOX) states that no company can take action in retaliation against individuals who report suspected illegal activities within the organization.

○ It is required that an organization adopt a written policy and establish procedures for handling employee and volunteer complaints.

○ The Dodd-Frank Wall Street Reform and Consumer Protection Act of 2010 added provisions to incentivize whistleblowers and to provide protection from retaliation.[32]

---

[31] ("Establishing a Code of Conduct for Nonprofit Board Members" by Lena Eisenstein [October 27, 2021]) BoardEffect https://www.boardeffect.com/blog/code-of-conduct-for-board-members/

[32] ("The Dodd-Frank Act and implications for nonprofit organizations" by Jonathan L. Pompan, Venable LLP [January 20, 2021]) Lexology https://www.lexology.com/library/detail.aspx?g=65b4f5d2-f6e2-4934-bd86-eaacb4c72db2

5. **Document Retention Policy**

   ○ Document retention and destruction policies outline the length of time your organization will keep certain documents and records, either in hard copy or electronic form. The policies serve as guidelines for staff and board members, indicating which documents to discard and which to save. Such policies ensure compliance with federal laws and prevent accidental or innocent destruction of records.[33]

6. **Non-disclosure Agreement**

   ○ This is signed by anyone in the organization that has access to private information the organization does not want its competition to have. It requires the signers to keep this information private while at the organization and for a specified time after leaving, and forbids them to start a competing organization with the information learned at the current organization.

7. **Non-discrimination Statement**

   ○ This states that your organization does not discriminate on the basis of the characteristics listed in the statement.

8. **Gender Policy**

   ○ If the mission of your organization caters specifically to one gender, it is necessary to define what gender means in your organization. Does it mean those who identify as that gender? Those who were listed on their birth certificate as that gender?

   ○ Do a search for the gender policies created for all-women's colleges to get a good idea of what you need to consider.

9. **Nepotism Policy**

   ○ Be clear as to where in your organization the close relatives (parent, child, spouse, or others you choose to include) of current employees or board members may or may not be employed or otherwise engaged, whether as a board member, vendor, or other.

---

[33] ("Document Retention and Destruction Policies for Nonprofit Organizations" [August 2010 Updated November 2011]) The Watershed Institute https://www.nypap.org/wp-content/uploads/2016/04/watershed_institute._document_policies_for_nonprofits.pdf

## Additional Policies and Helpful Tools:

1. **Director Letter of Commitment**
   - This document spells out what is expected from a board member and details what they can and cannot do in their board capacity.
   - Each director signs a Letter of Commitment at the **start of each new fiscal year**.

2. A **Board Roster** (spreadsheet) listing the names and contact information for all board members that also lists their occupations/employers, their board position, when they joined the board, when the current term ends, and when they are due to cycle off the board

3. An **Organizational (Org) Chart** that shows who reports to whom to make the chain of command clear (see Appendix V)

4. A **General Succession Plan**
   - At least in vague outline, this should be a plan for replacing key members of the team if, for any reason, they are no longer able to perform their duties.
   - Most importantly, there need to be plans in place for each key person to have a backup. The understudy should be learning the role to be able take over after the key person's term ends, or, in the case of an emergency replacement, to carry expertise and historical memory from the current board members to future members. Having the "Vice" or "Assistant" board roles that prepare for the role above them will help with this process.
   - You should be forming a plan to move the founder from a leading role to an advisory role in the future, bringing in the next generation.
   - When looking to replace the leader, look for a person who is passionate about the mission – someone who wants to further the initiatives put in place by the current leader.
   - Succession planning also includes keeping good records and "how to" documents for procedures and reporting, so the next person does not need to reinvent the wheel. Consider creating a manual with these important procedures all documented in one place.
   - Each key player should have a written outline of the work they do, kept in an easily accessible location, so someone else could take over if needed.
   - Record your organization's history and historical knowledge – consider keeping it in the cloud and in a few other places so it will never be lost.

## Failure of Succession

A Delaware nonprofit organization was started by a woman who was passionate about the mission. She was able to recruit a board, they did some projects, and they were able to obtain some funding for those projects. The founder was also chairing the board.

The founder/chair did the right thing and went to the Delaware Alliance for Nonprofit Advancement (DANA) for training through their workshops. Even though she had the passion, a good board, successful projects, funding, and nonprofit training, when it was time to look for a successor for her as board chair, no one on the board was willing to step up. She did not have any prospects for someone to take over leading the organization.

If the founder could not recruit someone from her own board to take over the leadership, this, unfortunately, may be a mission that is not of broad interest to the community. DANA members connected her with two other organizations that were somewhat similar to see about maybe merging their efforts.

The original nonprofit ended up shutting down its operations. This is a clear case where someone had a passion and was able to get people excited to about the mission early on, but, unfortunately, that was not enough for it to succeed in the long run. They did a lot right but were ultimately unable to form a sustainable succession plan.

5. **Enterprise Risk Management Plan**
   - Look at the risks you need to be aware of in all aspects of the organization – finances, talent, IT, governance – and consider what you will do if the worst happens.
   - If a large funding source you rely on dries up, how will you pivot?
   - Are there risks to moving to a database software program, and, if so, what are those risks and how will you deal with them?

6. **Policy & Procedures Manual**
   - Keep all policies and procedures together in one binder and saved "in the cloud" for easy access.
   - Give a copy to all members of the organization to whom they apply.

7. **Employee Handbook**

   ○ The handbook details the policies, rules, and benefits for employees. You may want to have a lawyer review it.

   ○ Give the handbook to new employees and ask them to sign to acknowledge they have received it and understand the contents.

8. **Life Experience**

   ○ This is rarely thought about in new or existing organizations, but there needs to be someone in charge on a daily basis who knows how to navigate and react when the unexpected happens.

   ○ It is great to train new, younger people, but they do need training and will need time and experience before running things on their own.

9. **Diversity, Equity, and Inclusion (DEI) and Other Board Training**

   ○ Training may be very helpful in creating a more inclusive and ethical environment. The board may need this guidance to become allies of traditionally marginalized or historically underrepresented groups within and outside your organization.

   ○ Consider joining a local nonprofit support organization (a member of the Center for Nonprofit Excellence or National Council of Nonprofits, or other organization that has a Standards for Excellence accreditation) that will offer board training and nonprofit certifications.

   ○ These organizations can help because, whatever your organization is going through, another nonprofit has had similar issues, and they can help you determine what course of action is best to correct the problem.

   ○ They can also help your organization match your mission to your policies and procedures.

## Professional Resources

Look at your needs for **paid employees or hired contractors.**

- You may be able to receive some pro bono help or services or trade for sponsorship advertising. If not, you may find a need to hire professionals.

- Each organization will be different, so look closely at your unique circumstances when considering where to fill the gaps to move your nonprofit forward.

**Some employees or contracting services you may need:**

- **Accountant or bookkeeper** to handle daily transactions and the books (this person should be bonded because they will be handling money and your financial records)
- **Certified Public Accountant (CPA)** to file taxes and other required filings and a **2$^{nd}$ independent CPA** to do an annual audit (they do not need to work for separate CPA firms)
- **Attorney** for any legal advice – the attorney offering legal advice/counsel should not be a board member and should have nonprofit expertise
- **Web Designer**
- **Social Media and Marketing**
- **Grant Writer**
- **IT Services**

**Consider:**

- If hiring professionals, find specialists for the area you need – not all attorneys have experience with nonprofit bylaws, and not all accountants are experts with 990 filings.
- Each state has dollar thresholds for when a nonprofit must be audited, but some funders may require an audit at lower thresholds to qualify for their funding. **When starting out, it may be possible to have a less-expensive financial compilation or review done instead of a full-fledged audit.**
- Be aware of the costs of salaries before you start a big hiring push because they will significantly impact your budget, and salaries not related to program staffing will take funds away from the mission work.
- Always remember that staff members, including the paid executive director (ED), are not board members. They may attend board meetings and give updates, but the employees report to the executive director who reports to the board, so the board should meet in Executive Session without them to discuss any staff-related issues.
- When the organization grows to the point of hiring staff members, consider a team approach rather than a hierarchy where the ED lords over the other staff members. (See more about this in Chapter 10.)
- Be sure to have human resources (HR) policies in place before your first hire so everyone knows the rules from the start.

- If your staff has bought in to the mission, is paid a decent salary, and has a board and ED that are responsive to and considerate of their needs, turnover will remain low, and you will not need to constantly work at hiring and training new employees. This will give the whole organization more time to focus on accomplishing the mission-related goals.

## Measuring Mission Impact

### Yoga 4 Change

A grassroots organization started offering trauma-informed yoga for people incarcerated in northeast Florida. From the beginning, they started tracking data. They measured changes in mood, levels of stress, and blood pressure before and after the yoga sessions, and the data was tracked using spreadsheets and manual systems. They collected the information for months and months, and the outcomes showed statistically significant impact of the Yoga 4 Change programs.

Because funders saw them passionately, albeit informally, tracking data and showing positive outcomes, they provided funding for a full-scale study with Boston University. Later, they entered into the University of North Florida, Data Science for Social Good program. The faculty and students worked together to create a proprietary data tracking management system. They hired two of those students as System Development Contractors to continue making improvements and updates to the system over time, and they are still on the Yoga 4 Change team.

The organization now has amazing data to bring to potential funders, and they have become a major player in the northeast Florida nonprofit space. They offer change by providing a purpose-driven yoga curriculum to veterans, individuals who are experiencing incarceration, youth, and people living with mental health conditions, and they now have multiple locations throughout Florida.

Being able to quantify the impact your organization is having on the community is important for a number of reasons. The most important reason is so you know whether what you are doing is working. Also, funders want to know how their money is being or will be spent, and they want to know if those funds are having the intended impact. These measurements will ultimately tell your story and will determine future funding.

Impact needs to be tracked and measured from the first offered program. You will need to decide how you track the data and how it will best be understood. Look at the expected outcomes and compare those with the actual outcomes. This can be done by measuring the number of people who completed your 6-week course, by looking at the results on a program-end survey of the participants, or by tracking how many students from your program went on from high school to college. Determine what key metrics you will track.

You can develop a **Theory of Change model** before starting a new project or program. Theory of Change defines how a given intervention is expected to lead to a specific change, so it is easier to find logical links between actions and outcomes. Create a detailed description of how and why the desired change is expected to happen and what progress and success will look like. Determine your long-term goals, measurable indicators of success, and actions to achieve those goals. Analyze the change theories for each program at regular intervals to measure success and to see if new theories and goals need to be put in place.

The business world tends to track sales, inventory, expenses, and income, but they do not track outcomes in the way a nonprofit needs to track them. If there are only business people on your board, it may not be obvious to them to take these steps, so this is another reason to have a diverse board. Many times, the work a nonprofit does is impactful, but the people who do the work do not know how to translate that into data.

Tracked data is needed to inform those who are not actually doing the work, so all can understand it. Those doing the work need to know what they should be tracking from the outset. Your local nonprofit support group can help train your staff and volunteers on outcomes and evaluations if you need help.

## Measuring Awareness

Chris Grundner started the Kelly Heinz-Grundner Brain Tumor Foundation (KHG) in 2005 after losing his wife at age 31, after her two-year battle with a brain tumor. Chris found there was no organization in the country at the time focused primarily on education and awareness about brain tumors, so he was determined to help get the word out.

In September 2008, the Foundation launched a three-month "Get Your Head in the Game!" public awareness campaign. Delaware billboards, bus signs, and a display at the Wilmington Amtrak station advertised facts about brain tumors.

All nonprofits need to measure outcomes of their programs. This is made more difficult when your program is an awareness organization rather than a program-driven organization. KHG was able to measure its progress by doing a baseline polling of people in public places, asking them specific questions about their awareness and knowledge about brain tumors before the campaign. After the three-month campaign ended, they conducted similar surveys and were able to measure a significant increase in the public's knowledge and awareness.

Because the campaign had measurable impact, they were able to get funding from the tobacco settlement fund and others to continue to grow their campaign efforts. KHG proved its usefulness to the public, and in 2012 it successfully merged with The Brain Tumor Society, a national organization.

## Improving the Overall Ecosystem

Your nonprofit organization is part of a larger ecosystem, so it should look at programming and support holistically. If you are working on improving the education system in your area, just changing the curriculum or how teachers work in the classrooms will not address all of what contributes to how children learn. If students come to school hungry or unhealthy or are living in a shelter, all of these factors weigh heavily on that individual child and will affect their ability to focus on schoolwork.

As your organization grows in the community, look into developing and fostering partnerships with groups who are working to improve other aspects that affect your constituents. Together you can make positive changes to the whole ecosystem to fix the problems, not just the symptoms.

**Feedback looping**, actually listening to the people you serve and implementing changes in response, is also very important. People like to feel they are a part of the missions that are meant to help them. If they feel unheard or unseen, there could be critical failures in delivering the mission.

## Know the Boundaries

A 501(c)(3) public charity is bound by many regulations. There are annual filing requirements that must be completed and filed on time to maintain charitable status. Nonprofits also need to know the boundaries if they choose to step into the political world.

You can and should advocate for your mission, and you may do legislative lobbying (to push for certain laws that will be beneficial to your mission) as long as that lobbying activity amounts to only an "insubstantial" amount of the nonprofit's activities. No definition for "insubstantial" has been provided by Congress or the IRS. This seems to be subjective and arbitrary, so the nonprofit has to be careful. You can file IRS Form 5768 (also known as taking the 501(h) election) that allows your organization to be measured by the more objective "expenditure test" if you do not spend a large portion of your budget on lobbying efforts.

A nonprofit may not back a particular candidate for office, or it is in danger of losing its 501(c)(3) nonprofit status. The IRS says:

"Under the Internal Revenue Code, all section 501(c)(3) organizations are absolutely **prohibited from** directly or indirectly participating in, or intervening in, any **political campaign on behalf of** (or in opposition to) **any candidate for elective public office**. Contributions to political campaign funds or public statements of position (verbal or written) made on behalf of the organization in favor of or in opposition to any candidate for public office clearly violate the prohibition against political campaign activity. Violating this prohibition may result in denial or revocation of tax-exempt status and the imposition of certain excise taxes.

"Certain activities or expenditures may not be prohibited depending on the facts and circumstances. For example, certain voter education activities (including presenting public forums and publishing voter education guides) conducted in a non-partisan manner do not constitute prohibited political campaign activity. In addition, other activities intended to encourage people to participate in the electoral process, such as voter registration and get-out-the-vote drives, would not be prohibited political campaign activity if conducted in a non-partisan manner.

"On the other hand, voter education or registration activities with evidence of bias that (a) would favor one candidate over another; (b) oppose a candidate in some manner; or (c) have the effect of favoring a candidate or group of candidates, will constitute prohibited participation or intervention."[34]

---

[34] ("The Restriction of Political Campaign Intervention by Section 501(c)(3) Tax-Exempt Organizations" [Updated June 17, 2022]) IRS.gov https://www.irs.gov/charities-non-profits/charitable-organizations/the-restriction-of-political-campaign-intervention-by-section-501c3-tax-exempt-organizations

## Advisory Council

You may want to add an Advisory Council (AC) that can give advice and help you make connections. The AC should be made up of people who are passionate about your mission, are very connected in the community, maybe have some business or political contacts, and/or are very accomplished in the areas where you need the most help. These people would probably be great board members, but they may be too busy or travel too much to serve on your board. The AC is also a good place for friends, family members, or others who cycle off the board of directors but who you want to remain engaged.

Keep the AC abreast of organizational news with email updates, quarterly e-newsletters, and biannual AC meetings to keep them energized and backing your cause. You should also invite them to attend your regular board meetings, but this should be optional. Be sure to ask directly for help in areas of their expertise or connections. If you are looking for a new board or AC member with a particular skillset, need ideas on how to keep existing donors engaged or attract new donors, or if you are wondering how best to qualify for a grant or sponsorship from their company, ask for their advice.

## Committees

Committees do the "boots on the ground" behind-the-scenes work that there is not time to tackle in a board meeting. They can be charged with looking at the overall financial picture, getting the word out about your organization, researching new options or new ways to deliver your mission, and a host of other things. If it is a research committee, once the research is complete, the committee chair can bring the findings to the board to further discuss and possibly implement.

Committee service can be an on-ramp to serving on the board, or it can be a way to retain good, strong, passionate people once their board term expires. There are many different types of committees. Some may be **standing** (open-ended and longer term), and some may be **ad-hoc** (for a specific short-term purpose when the board needs something to be looked at in more detail). These temporary committees may be shut down when the issue is resolved or the event has taken place, or the board may find a need to make a temporary committee permanent.

A committee, in most cases, should be led by an existing board member, and the committee members may be a combination of other board members and community volunteers. Look for people with expertise in the needed area. Try to avoid appointing a committee chair or committee member without buy-in from the appointee, or they may not lead with enthusiasm.

Examples of the many and varied **types of committees** include, but are not limited to:

- Financial/Investment
- Governance/Nominating
- Strategic Planning
- Insurance
- Grants and Post Grants (if a granting organization)
- Development/Fundraising
- Executive Compensation
- Event Planning
- Social Media/Marketing
- Volunteer Coordination

## Volunteers

Volunteers come in all shapes, sizes, and reasons for assisting. In some cases, a local corporation will require its employees to either take part in a "volunteer day" by lending a hand to an organization of the employee's choosing, or they may coordinate efforts with your nonprofit and ask their employees to do specific events with and for you. Some volunteers will show up from the local community and want to help, while others may be recruited family members or friends of people within the organization.

"Corporate volunteers" can be beneficial in the short run, but they most likely have no affinity for your organization. They may show up because their company is excited about your project, because it is a day off for them or a company-sponsored project, or maybe it is a team-building exercise for them and their co-workers. It is possible to turn corporate volunteers into "friends" if they come to value the work you are doing and want to help.

On the other hand, your "friends & family volunteers" will be the people you can count on to show up. They will speak on behalf of your organization if you need them to, and will extoll your virtues.

If you have a mixture of older and younger or experienced and less-experienced volunteers, the tasks each is able to accomplish may vary. Younger people may be able to do more physical tasks and remain on their feet for a longer time. The older people may be less physical but have the advantage of their life experience to help them reason out ways to overcome a difficult obstacle. There may also be a gap in how they approach a task or their technical knowledge and capacity. You may want to think ahead about how they may work together to get the job done.

It is important that all of the volunteers have a good experience, see the passion and mission of the organization, and not only want to come back again, but they want to bring other volunteers with them the next time. Even corporate employees who are "voluntold" by their company to help your nonprofit will want to return if the experience is something that makes a difference in their lives.

There are myriad ways to try to accomplish this. If you are holding an outside event, and the weather is not cooperating, volunteers may still enjoy the music a DJ is playing that has them dancing in the rain. Provide some food and drinks if they will be there for a long time or at meal times. Simply preparing for the volunteers so that everyone has a name tag, knows what jobs need to be completed, and knows who to go to if they have questions or need more work, will go a long way to keep volunteers from feeling like they are not needed or valued. If there is someone who looks lost or alone, be sure to speak to them and introduce them to other friendly souls they can work alongside. Let them know that their help is desired and appreciated.

After a volunteer event, and this cannot be stated enough, remember to thank each and every volunteer and let them know how much the work they did matters to your nonprofit. Be sure to capture all names and contact information so you can thank them via email and invite them to future events and volunteer opportunities.

Happy volunteers who see the good work being done, who feel good about themselves after helping, will be your sales force in the community. They will be the ones to sell your mission to others.

## Safety Plan

None of us like to think about worst-case scenarios, but it is important to have plans in place for staff members and volunteers to follow if a situation arises. First, do a risk assessment and consider the types of safety hazards your employees and volunteers may encounter. Next, adopt safety policies for guidance when an issue arises.

**Implement the policies:**

- Eliminate physical hazards (if you have a physical location or standard meeting space).
- Offer safety training.

- Review insurance coverage.
- Create a reporting system so staff and volunteers have a standard procedure for reporting hazards, injuries, illnesses, or incidents – including close calls – without fear of retaliation.
- Prepare for emergencies by conducting drills (fire, active shooter, weather threats) and create an evacuation plan.
- Do a new risk assessment each time you create new programs or services.
- Investigate accidents and injuries to determine if there is a way to prevent future troubles.
- Measure results by tracking improved safety and reductions in accidents, sick days, medical expenses, workers' compensation premiums, and work hours lost to injury.

**Prevent violence and harassment:**

- Keep basic safety in mind. Look for office space with security features like lighted parking lots, security cameras, alarm systems, and make sure no employee is working alone or walking to their car alone in an unsafe area.
- Create a zero-tolerance policy for harassment.
- Be alert to weapons. Inspect work areas for objects that could be used as weapons and remove as many as possible, especially in areas that are open to the public.
- Make it easy to report threats or violent incidents.
- Train staff members and volunteers in self-defense.
- Encourage peaceful conflict resolution.

## Crisis Plan

No organization wants to have a crisis or even think about having one. For the same reasons you pay for insurance, you should have a well-thought-out crisis plan with specific steps to take that you can start to implement the day that it happens. A crisis may take the form of the sudden need to relieve a staff person or even the director of their duties, a wrongful termination suit, a rogue volunteer with a negative accusation, a data breach, an employee or board member embezzling or committing other financial misconduct, a benefactor scandal, board defection by a minority or majority of the members, or any other issues that shed a negative light on your organization.

When you are in the midst of the crisis, you may not be thinking clearly, but you can follow these steps to not only help you through it, but also to help mitigate any future problems that could come with handling a situation poorly. People will forgive you if you are honest and forthcoming from the start.

**The organization leaders should keep this list in their desk drawers so they may pull it out, clear their heads, and quickly start to activate in a moment of crisis[35]:**

1. Determine if law enforcement needs to be involved. If so, you want them involved from the very beginning. The public perception of the situation will be more favorable if your first call is to law enforcement, should the situation require it.

2. Identify any relevant witnesses and/or documents. Make a list of them, and start to interview the witnesses. More than one person from your organization should be present at each interview, and a written statement should be taken. Video of the interview could be very helpful if the witness is willing to be recorded. You may want to enlist an attorney at this point to help guide the interviews.

3. If needed, promptly and without bias, retain an internal investigator. "Internal" does not mean a person within the organization. This should be an independent person outside of your organization – maybe a former FBI agent or former prosecutor – who will look at and gather all pertinent information and evidence.

4. Determine if this is a matter where your insurance may come into play. Does the behavior trigger the Directors & Officers policy or the general liability policy? If so, your insurance carrier should be notified of the situation right away. There is no harm in putting your insurance carrier on notice.

5. Initiate a legal hold (also known as a litigation hold). Instruct all in your organization that no documents or electronically stored information (ESI) are to be discarded or destroyed. This is done because there may be information relevant to the case, but also to avoid the appearance of attempting to hide evidence.

---

[35] List from Mark Reardon, attorney and nonprofit board leader

6. Swiftly implement a Communication Plan within your organization. Make it clear that any texts, emails, or other notes sent by members of your organization may be used as evidence later, so do not discuss the details of the issue with anyone (other than legal counsel) in written form. No one besides the person chosen in number 7 below should speak to the press or anyone else about the matter.

7. Identify and train the appropriate voice and face of the organization to confront the issue. This is the person who will communicate with all of your stakeholders (staff, board, benefactors) as well as the press and other outside factions. In many cases, this may be the president/CEO, but there are times when a different communications person is needed. The situation may call for a paid media professional. Rarely is a lawyer the correct person to be the voice of the organization.

Facing a crisis or negative assertion in no way means that your whole organization is "bad." Bad things happen to good organizations, and, if they handle them the right way, they can make a full recovery.

**Also Important:**

The day-to-day operations will be very full with many of the same things needed to run a successful for-profit business. If you do the little things right, you may be able to successfully keep big problems from arising.

♦ **Work at attracting the right people to your organization.** You will find that if you directly ask a person of influence for their help, it is too easy for them to turn you down. They will have many excuses about being too busy or it not being the right fit. But if you ask them for their advice on how you can do something and what they see as your biggest challenges, they will "own" their advice and will most likely be more willing to help execute the plan. Ask them to use their hands or their mind first, then think about asking for additional donations later.

♦ Consider an organization-wide **group calendar** or calendars to track things like **strategic communications**, important **upcoming events, board and AC meeting dates**, and other relevant information. There are online platforms that make this easy. (See Chapter 11 for some options.)

♦ Strongly consider **background checks** for staff members and regular volunteers. This will help to alleviate your organization's risk factors, especially if you work closely with youth or other vulnerable populations. In some jurisdictions, this will be required.

- Realize that even when you have a leader who is great, they may not be great at everything. There was an instance where, when the executive director left after ten years, the board discovered the payroll taxes had not been paid for any of those years, and they really had to dig themselves out of a hole. **Be aware of the oversight and support your organization needs to function properly in all areas.**

- **Make time to remind yourself and your team of your "why."** When you are dealing with the daily minutiae, it is easy to lose sight of who you are helping and why you are investing so much of yourself in the organization. At staff or board meetings, regularly build in time to read a thank you letter or a quote from someone whose life you have made better because of the time and effort you have invested.

In the next chapter we will look at all things financial, including the business practices of issuing a Request for Proposal (RFP) for vendors' products or services, bookkeeping and audits of the financial records, and fundraising.

CHAPTER 8

# MONEY MATTERS!

⸻ • ◦ ● ◦ • ⸻

*"You always need more funding than you realize."*

Stephanie Cory
(Nonprofit Consultant)

"No margin, no mission" is an important mantra for any nonprofit organization. Your mission is the goal you are all striving to reach, but, without funding, your mission cannot be accomplished or even tended to. As a nonprofit, your immediate goal is fulfilling your mission. However, you need to generate funding that can be funneled to that mission.

In many ways, running a nonprofit is harder than running a for-profit business because a nonprofit has that "double bottom line" burden where, to be successful, you need to be achieving your mission AND your finances need to be in the black (more coming in than going out). If you have one without the other, the organization will be hard-pressed to thrive and survive.

Funders will be looking at what percentage of the money you raise each year goes directly to your mission. Some people believe that "to raise money, you have to spend money," and, while that may be true to an extent, in the nonprofit world, overhead needs to be kept in check. Your potential donors will not be inclined to give you more money because they have seen your elegantly-appointed offices with fancy furnishings. In fact, the opposite may be true if they are concerned you are not distributing your funding to the community you are serving.

The funds your organization is entrusted with are public funds (the reason you qualify for tax-exempt status), not your personal funds, so be sure there is clear delineation.

The majority of the board members, not just a few outspoken outliers, need to be in agreement as to how they are spent. The focus should be mission-driven.

The board has a fiduciary duty to exercise care in how the organization's funds are being used. It is important for the board to have financial information that is current to allow them to make their decisions. Sometimes it is difficult for the treasurer to get updated financial information when they rely on a secondary source (financial institution or a committee member who has not yet processed all of the event income and expenses), but they should strive to present up-to-date financials at least quarterly.

## Checks & Balances

Checks and balances should be built into all that you do. There should be processes in place that require a different person for each step of the money trail. If you do an online search for "Nonprofit Embezzlement" you will find hundreds of examples of trusted staff members or volunteers helping themselves to the nonprofit's assets until they got caught. You want to believe that all who handle the valuables in your organization will do the right thing, but people are human, and there are all sorts of reasons people stick their hand in the cookie jar, especially if the lack of procedures makes following through on the temptation easy.

The person who opens the mail should record what has been received, then hand off cash, checks, and credit card donations to the bookkeeper who processes them. Someone else should be tasked with making the bank deposits. If you have online donations, the person who processes the payments should not be the only person with access to the online payment accounts.

Require two signatures on each check for expenses and a board vote for expenditures over an agreed-upon dollar amount. Decide who in the organization will have access to online bank accounts, and be sure that there are checks and balances in place. If there are credit cards for purchases, entrust someone in your organization with keeping a close eye on the types of expenditures to be sure there are no personal or extravagant charges.

There should be very limited access and ability to transfer funds. The treasurer needs to be able to reconcile the amounts recorded as coming in and going out with the bank balance and other financial records.

Have protocols in place to immediately handle any misuse or even the appearance of money mishandling. Your organization's reputation and future funding depend on everything being above board.

An organization founder may be tempted to infuse the nonprofit with their own money to cover up an error or misuse of funds. They may try to hide it from the board and others in the organization. This is never okay, and it should be easily uncovered with an annual audit.

A nonprofit organization is a business. Even if making a profit is not its main goal, keeping a close eye on the funds is crucial.

## Budget

A budget is not just an indefinite aim for high income and low expenses. A lot of thought needs to go into planning the budget for the fiscal year. Each committee (for all-volunteer organizations) or cost center/program should look carefully at what funds it realistically thinks it can bring into the organization while also looking realistically at the costs of doing business for the next fiscal year. These numbers should be compiled into an overall budget for the organization by the person responsible for managing the finances. The finance manager will then present the budget to the board.

This should give the board enough information to make decisions about where to cut or increase spending, taking into consideration the nonprofit's mission and strategic plan. They may also contemplate whether and how to use any board-designated unrestricted reserve funds that have accumulated.

The board will review the final budget numbers at a meeting (where a quorum is present) before the start of the new fiscal year and vote to adopt the budget. Your bylaws should state whether the budget approval needs to be by majority or supermajority vote.

## Building the Budget

For the first year, the budget will be your best guess as to your 12-month financial picture. After the first year, an analysis should be done as to what the actual income and expenses were for the past fiscal year, what changes you know will be coming up in the next year (a grant you got last year that you are not eligible for again, an increase in fees or utilities, etc.), and other projections you can make to come up with an accurate prediction for the next year.

Break these analyses down by committee or section of the organization so the stakeholders in each area are the ones making the predictions, as they will have the most knowledge and experience in that area, and this process will help them "buy in" to meeting their predictions. The treasurer can use these numbers to compile an organization-wide budget combining all of the smaller section budgets, remembering to also include operations costs and other income that do not relate to a specific cost center.

Every effort should be made in each committee and the overall organization to stay within the budgeted expense numbers (or stay under them) and to reach for the income goals (or exceed them). If you are realistic about what is possible when forming the annual budget, it should not be hard to do. There may be certain unexpected expenses, but maybe the committee can find a way to offset that by decreasing another expense. If one grant that you were counting on did not come through, look at other grant opportunities for which you may qualify.

The goal is to have a balanced budget each fiscal year where the expenses are less than or equal to the income. There may be some years, however, that the board agrees to deficit spend (go "in the red," or spend more than the income) to invest in the future of the organization. This is forward-thinking strategy that should be weighed carefully. If it will truly increase the capacity of the organization to serve its mission, funders should understand the temporary deficit.

An updated budget/financial statement should be presented to the board at every board meeting that clearly shows all income and expenses that have occurred since the last meeting. It is important to monitor the budget vs. actual income and expenses. This way you can make changes and adjust as needed throughout the fiscal year in an attempt to have a balanced budget at the end of the year.

**A good budget will show:**

- **Income** that is broken down by types:
  - ○ Program fees
  - ○ Annual campaign
  - ○ Grants
  - ○ Individual donations
  - ○ Miscellaneous donations
  - ○ In-kind contributions
  - ○ Event income (broken down by event tickets, sponsorships, raffle or other event sales, event donations)
  - ○ Interest Income
  - ○ Income specific to your organization

- **Expenses** divided into sections:
  - ○ Programming – any items that go directly toward your mission and those you serve (the breakdown under each program can be as specific as needed to make comparisons year-to-year)
  - ○ Fundraising – printing and mailing the annual campaign fundraising letter, credit card fees paid when a donor pays by credit card, letterhead and envelope printing with logo and address specific to fundraising efforts
  - ○ Event – any expenses incurred to plan or run your event(s)
  - ○ Administrative (not related to programs) – salaries, contractor support, office rent or mortgage, utilities, database, online presence fees, nonprofit group memberships, franchise taxes, post office box, insurance, bank fees, letterhead and envelope printing for general thank you letter or other purposes, marketing & communications spending for the overall organization

**The columns in the Year-to-Date budget report[36] should show (columns listed below in order from left to right):**

1. Income and expense descriptions
2. The agreed-upon budget numbers for the whole fiscal year for each item
3. Actual totals for each item year-to-date
4. Actual-to-Budget percentage (e.g. the board can easily see the organization has only spent 52% of the amount budgeted for the year for marketing appeals, and this meeting is taking place eight months into the fiscal year, so they still have 48% of the total budget that may be spent over the next four months, OR, the board can see that insurance was much more expensive than they predicted and is at 120% of the total budgeted, so maybe they should look at ways to save that amount in some other category)
5. Actual income and expense numbers from the prior fiscal year to see how the numbers compare
6. Actual income and expense numbers from two years ago to see the progression

The organization should be planning its budget for the next year, but some grant applications will require you to look at income and expenses for the next three

---

[36] There is a sample budget sheet in Appendix VI

years. You should be able to reasonably extrapolate from current and past numbers to give a good estimate.

## Costs of Doing Business

Even though a public charity is tax-exempt, that does not mean it will not have a lot of operating expenses. As mentioned earlier, running a nonprofit, in many ways, is like running a for-profit business. This is especially true when looking at the expense side.

When requesting funding, do not forget to include the operating costs associated with a project. Of course, you want to be able to show that the majority of your funding goes directly to your mission work, but all of that has associated costs, so make sure you are requesting all that you need to run the whole project. This includes the cost of keeping the lights on, accounting or other software, and staff time committed to the project. Determine the man-hours needed to run the project, and add the cost per hour to your funding request.

Below are some (but unfortunately not all) of the costs associated with running a nonprofit. Each organization is unique and will have its own set of expenses that may or may not include the following:

- Set-up fees – filing fees to incorporate; to hire a nonprofit attorney or accountant to create the Nonstock Charter (if required) and bylaws, obtain an EIN, set up the organization's incorporation, 501(c)(3) status (some of these may be done without hiring an attorney or accountant)
- Registered Agent fees (if you choose to hire a registered agent, they may be able to do the initial corporate formation work for you)
- Fees for domain name, website, and email addresses linked to domain name
- Subscription fees for accounting software, communications software, payment processing, a survey site, etc.
- Office supplies
- Printing
- Mailings
- Post office box
- Marketing/Advertising (including targeted ads on social media)
- Meeting space (if there is no physical office location)
- Rent or mortgage

- Utilities
- Affiliate fees if your nonprofit is a chapter of a national organization
- Fundraiser event expenses
- Credit card fees
- Insurance – Directors & Officers (D&O), general liability, employer's liability, workers' compensation, health insurance, professional liability, abuse and molestation liability, Key Man (insuring a larger-than-life key person – founder, CEO, executive director – who would be hard to replace if they unexpectedly went missing)
- Membership fees for nonprofit support organization(s)
- Payroll, tax filings, administrative help, independent contractors
- Fees to file to solicit funds in your state or other states
- Legal fees
- Bank fees
- Annual franchise tax fee (if required)
- Audited Financial Statement (if required by grantor or one of the states where you are registered to solicit funds) OR the less expensive but less detailed and less comprehensive Compilation Financial Statement

As the organization grows and starts to hire staff members, the **employee salaries** could become the largest expense. Be sure to research competitive salary ranges for your sector before hiring. (See more about this in Chapter 10.)

Be cognizant that you "get what you pay for," so your organization needs to offer all employees a salary they can live on and be reasonable in the hours you expect them to work for that wage. If your workers are passionate about the work and are treated fairly, they will reward you with many years of loyalty.

Remember that the organization is tax-exempt, but the **salaries your nonprofit pays to employees are not exempt from taxes!** All of the withholdings required for a for-profit company are also required when a nonprofit pays salaries.

Funders will be looking at what percentage of your budget goes directly to programming. Many of the operating expenses listed above are not going directly to those you serve. You should aim for 75-90% of your total expenses to go directly to your mission.

To make this a bit clearer, consider that your operating expenses, including salaries, total $100,000. This means that at least $300,000 of your total expenses should go directly toward programming and those you serve. In this scenario, total salaries are less than $100,000 (which, depending on the number of employees you are paying, may not provide a living wage for them), and total income must be a minimum of $400,000 to have a balanced budget.

It is a bit sobering to think about hiring people with this in mind. The $100,000 above includes not only salaries, but also the withholdings for employees plus any of the operating expenses from the menu above. Think about hiring employees who will not only help you with the programming, but who will also help to increase income in some way to assist with covering those increased operating costs.

The organization's funds are, in essence, the community's funds, so every effort should be made to be fiscally responsible and, at the same time, transparent about how the funds are spent. You will have valid expenses, but there is a line that must not be crossed. Personal trips or items should never be paid for with the charity's funds. Every effort should be made to find sponsors for celebrations to thank volunteers or those that you serve, so the events are paid for with funds donated specifically for that purpose. That way you are able to honor your people and keep up morale while not using funds earmarked for programs. Good judgement goes a long way in preventing future scandals.

### Financial Statements

When your organization is just starting out, your financial statements will consist of a **budget sheet** and a **balance sheet** that gives a snapshot showing your organization's liquidity and cash position at a particular moment. For nonprofits, this balance sheet is often called a **statement of financial position.**

As you grow, your financial statements will also include an **income statement** (called a **statement of activities** for a nonprofit organization), a **statement of cash flows**, and a **statement of functional expenses** that shows the expenses of each functional area of your organization. Your accountant will be able to help you create and maintain these statements.

### Chasing Funding

A nonprofit's board, staff, and volunteers will spend a large percentage of their time looking for funding options, brainstorming ways to increase funding, and planning events to hopefully bring in funding. In most cases, it takes a great deal of income to serve your mission. The aim is to have a nest egg in liquid assets equivalent to at least two years of operating expenses to carry the organization through unexpected lean times.

Antithetical to the "if you build it, they will come" theory of nonprofit funding, in most cases it will take a few years of successful programming to be eligible to apply for grants or to attract other funders. In the early years your income may come mostly from annual appeals sent to individual donors and from fundraising events. Some organizations will have a model where they are able to charge membership fees. Others may get grants from corporations and foundations as they grow and build and have programming success to tout. Using only one avenue for funding will not be enough to be sustainable unless your organization remains very small.

Your organization should not rely solely on funding from a few sources with deep pockets because you will find yourself in trouble if one or more of them dries up unexpectedly. In Chapter 10 we will look at how, as your organization grows, contributing to an endowment fund will also bring in future funds from its earnings.

**A nonprofit should have a fundraising pyramid[37] like this:**

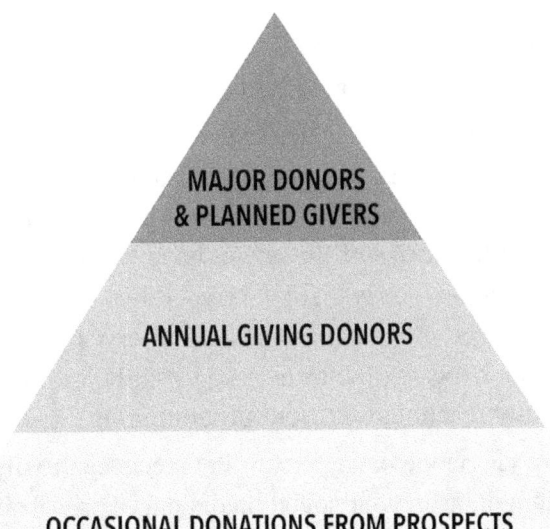

[37] This pyramid looks exclusively at individual donations and does not include funding from other sources such as corporate or foundation grants.

The base is made up of occasional donations from prospects, where the donations amass to form a good foundation. The center of the pyramid is your annual giving donors who reliably donate every year. At the top of the pyramid are major donors and planned givers (those who have designated a donation in their will) that your organization has worked hard to cultivate as "believers" in the work you are doing.

Nonprofit development (the act of building relationships with donors and the community[38]) should be approached using exceptional sales skills:

1. Always be on the lookout for **prospects.**

2. **Network, Network, Network!** Attend local events and introduce yourself to as many people as possible. Purchase a reusable name tag with your nonprofit's logo that will be a good conversation starter and will help people remember you and your organization. Get a small batch of business cards printed with your logo, website, and contact information that you can hand out to people you meet. Start to create relationships with all different types of people who may become your supporters.

3. **Sell yourself first**, then sell the mission and organization. If they like you, they are more likely to donate.

4. **Treat all prospects with respect**.

5. **Do not make any pre-conceived assumptions about a person's ability to give.** (Do not judge a book by its cover.)

6. Give the **elevator pitch** about the organization, making sure to read your audience. Some people may need you to tug at their heartstrings, and they will be swayed by stories of those you have helped or aim to help. Others may be detail people who want to get right down to what percentage of your funding goes directly to the mission, what reserves you have in the bank for lean times, which local influencers are on your board, and how many people you are actually reaching with your programming.

7. **Ask directly** via phone or in person. Prospects can easily ignore a plea for funds in an email or on your social media pages or website. It is not as easy to say no when someone looks them in the eye and asks with a smile.

8. Listen to their **objections** and try to overcome them – gently. You should start to anticipate the standard objections and have responses ready.

---

[38] ("Nonprofit Development: What Is It & How to Get a Job in It" [2022]) Scion Nonprofit https://scionnonprofitstaffing.com/nonprofit-development-what-is-it-how-to-get-job/

9. Leave each person you touch with a **favorable impression** of you and your organization. Even if they do not plan to donate today, they may remember you and choose to donate or get involved in the future.

10. **FOLLOW UP!** If you have told them you will reach out again, or if their employer requires you to fill out a form to release a matching gift, do not lose your opportunity by forgetting to dot the I's and cross the T's. If you make them beg you to take their money this time, there will probably not be a next time.

11. Be sure to send hand-written, personalized **thank you notes** to each donor explaining how their funds will be used and reminding them that they are making a difference.

If you work hard to maintain past and present income sources by making each person, corporation, or foundation feel appreciated with timely thank you letters, mentions in press releases and annual reports, and maybe even an annual phone call, they may become your top-tier donors. In the meantime, always be looking for new funding options.

Make prospecting a centralized effort rather than inadvertently having multiple people in your organization hitting up the same prospects over and over. Coordinate outreach (emails to sponsors, donation or volunteer requests, event invitations) rather than allowing multiple "silos" to all work autonomously, while duplicating efforts and possibly annoying your donors.

## Should We Accept?

Your board should approve a Donation Acceptance Policy or Gift Acceptance Policy[39] that provides structure and spells out what types of donations your organization will and will not accept. This way, there is no confusion or uncertainty when a questionable donation is proposed. The policy should include the forms of donations such as property, stocks, or crypto currency you will accept. E*TRADE[40] and TD Ameritrade[41] are two options for accepting and selling stock donations, and The Giving Block[42] is a sort of clearing house for crypto currency donations to nonprofits.

---

[39] ("Gift Acceptance Policies" [2022]) National Council of Nonprofits (Reprinted with permission from the National Council of Nonprofits.) https://www.councilofnonprofits.org/tools-resources/gift-acceptance-policies

[40] https://us.etrade.com/home

[41] https://www.tdameritrade.com/

[42] https://thegivingblock.com/#menu-about

The Donation Acceptance Policy should be clear as to how a donation from a person of questionable reputation is handled. What qualifies as a "questionable" reputation? Will you accept gifts from companies or individuals that are known to be the antithesis of your organization's values? Of course, some things cannot be anticipated, even with the best planning, so this policy will need to be revisited when a new situation arises that was not previously addressed in the policy.

One nonprofit had a lot of explaining to do when it came to light that they had accepted hundreds of thousands of dollars in donations from convicted sex offender and financier Jeffrey Epstein. *The New Yorker* revealed in 2019 how the organization had marked donations as anonymous and concealed his identity in calendar meetings with the nonprofit director.[43] This led to the resignation of the nonprofit director days after the article was published. Other nonprofits did not accept or had returned Epstein's donations. This would have been a much better choice than accepting funds from a person with questionable character, trying to be deceptive about where the funds came from, then being found out and lambasted in the press.

It may be very tempting to accept funds from a willing donor, even if there are strings attached. The donor may want your organization to stretch itself outside the limits of its mission to take on something new. **The board should be very clear as to the mission and values of the charity and not be seduced into changing the essence of them by the offer of much-needed funds.** They should stand firm and stick to quality fundraising that is always above board and on brand for the organization. It may not seem like it in the short run, but this will serve the organization well as it evolves and grows.

---

[43] ("How an Élite University Research Center Concealed Its Relationship with Jeffrey Epstein" by Ronan Farrow [September 6, 2019]) NewYorker.com https://www.newyorker.com/news/news-desk/how-an-elite-university-research-center-concealed-its-relationship-with-jeffrey-epstein

## The Hedgehog Concept

Jim Collins talks about the "Hedgehog Concept" in his book *Good to Great and the Social Sectors*[44]. It shows that your organization's sweet spot is where the concentric circles of, 1) what you are deeply passionate about, 2) what you can be best in the world at, and 3) what drives your resource engine, meet. This is where your nonprofit will achieve greatness.

You begin with passion, then assess what your organization can best contribute to the communities you touch (the unique area where your nonprofit can be better than any other organization). When you find and refine these two, you create a way to tie your resource engine (time, money, and brand) to the other two circles. Where they intersect is where you will do best.

"Time" is how well you attract people willing to contribute their efforts for free or at rates below what their talents yield in business. "Money" is your sustained cash flow, while "Brand" is how well your organization can cultivate a deep well of emotional goodwill and mind-share opportunities of potential supporters. If any of these components do not fit with or are somehow at odds with your mission (passion) or with what you are best in the world at (or at least in your region), be willing and able to turn them down.

This concept emphasizes exercising the discipline to say, "No, thank you" to opportunities that fail the hedgehog test. When resource engine components – time or money offered to you – do not fit with where your circles intersect, it is best to turn them down.

## Other Donation Considerations:

- Create a donation receipt letter that you send out to donors (required for cash donations of $250 or more) or hand to anyone requesting a donation receipt. Be sure to include:
  - Nonprofit name and logo
  - Nonprofit mailing address and EIN number
  - Statement that you are 501(c)(3) nonprofit
  - Donor name

---

[44] Collins, Jim *Good to Great and the Social Sectors: A Monograph to Accompany Good to Great* 2005

- ○ Date of donation
- ○ Amount of cash donation
- ○ Description of non-cash donation (do not assign a value)
- ○ Description and estimate of value of any goods or services your organization provided in exchange for the contribution OR a statement that no goods were exchanged

Be sure to check with your state and local government for any additional requirements.

- If your organization accepts donations that are restricted to use for specific purposes, the Financial Accounting Standards Board (FASB) has specific terminology and accounting processes to show this in your books. Check with your CPA if you accept restricted donations to be sure you are accounting for them properly.

- There may be a time when a donor would like to gift a building or other property. It may be a very generous donation, but your organization will need to carefully consider whether or not to accept it. There may be strings attached as to how long you need to hold onto it before you are free to sell it. It may be that the donor was not able to easily sell it for its appraised value, so it was more advantageous for them to donate it to your charity and take the appraised value as a tax write-off. This could mean that the property is older or in disrepair.

  Even if the property is not run down when gifted, you will need extra funding for its upkeep. A lawn will need to be mowed, the heat will need to be run so the pipes do not freeze in the winter, and repairs will need to be made as problems arise. Try to negotiate with the donor to add an endowment or other funds designated for future related expenses.

  The property may not be useful at all to the daily running of your organization. The board must weigh the pros and cons of accepting this type of gift.

### Solicitations

Donor solicitations should be carefully thought out and only sent once or twice a year via mail or email. You do not want to offend the donors by looking like you are constantly hounding them for more and more.

Some people will be turned off if the organization sends them items in the mail in the hope that the gifts will motivate them to "pay" for the items received. It can have the opposite effect in that potential donors may feel your organization wastes funds on these items rather than funding its mission. Others may feel more inclined to donate if they receive a free token of appreciation up front. Once your prospect list is large enough (over 1,000 contacts), you may want to do an **A/B test** where you divide your list in some way and send the item to half of the list and only a glossy brochure or solicitation letter to the other half. Then measure the results to see which worked best. Find ways to mark the responses that will be returned in the mail with donations, and create two separate links for online donations, so you are able to clearly measure which strategy brought in more funds.

Even though you want to keep your targeted asks to a minimum, ALWAYS make it easy for someone to add a donation when they visit your website or social media page. Add a "Donate" button to your page, an option to make an additional donation when signing up for your event, and have donation envelopes or card swipers available at events for optional donations. When people read or hear the emotional stories about who you are serving and why, they will be moved to give because they see you are doing good work.

Your donors, like most other humans, want to feel appreciated. Be sure to have an auto-response to an online donation that thanks them for helping those you serve, and send an official tax letter acknowledging the amount of the donation with a short explanation of how their funds will be used. It should be a priority to get the letters out to people within 48 hours of when the donation was received. If you are short-staffed and this is not possible, it should take no longer than a few weeks to thank them.

If you track how your funds are being used, are able to produce an accurate and verifiable record of how funds were spent, can show the impact these expenditures have had on the community, and keep it all transparent, donors will know they are helping you make a difference. This is what will bring in new donors, and it will help you retain donors who believe in your cause.

## Compliance

Nonprofits are required to comply with local, state, and federal laws and regulations or they may risk losing their tax-exempt status or other adverse consequences. As mentioned above, they need to pay payroll taxes and unemployment taxes like for-profit companies.[45]

---

[45] Churches are exempt from paying unemployment taxes, but this means their employees are not eligible to collect unemployment benefits. (There were exceptions during the pandemic.)

Each year nonprofits are required to file a Form 990 tax return with the IRS. It may be a 990-N (if gross receipts are under $50,000), a 990-EZ (gross receipts $50,000-$200,000), or a 990 (gross receipts over $200,000 or total assets over $500,000). No taxes will be due, but the longer 990 form is twelve pages long and asks for quite a lot of information. With the required attached schedules, it can grow to about 40 pages. The Sarbanes-Oxley Act of 2002 added questions to the 990 to be sure nonprofits are complying with the Act's requirements for a Whistleblower policy and document retention. Tax-exempt status may be withdrawn at any time if the IRS suspects any wrongdoing or finds problems. If you miss filing your 990 for three years, you could lose your 501(c)(3) status and would need to start at the beginning to reinstate it.

All board members should study the 990 of a large nonprofit to know what information is required and to be sure they each understand the 990 form. The 990s for all large nonprofits may be found online.[46]

A state franchise or incorporation tax report and fee (if applicable) will also be due each year. Each state has its own laws regulating what a nonprofit may do, what it must do to be a legal nonprofit entity in that state, and how it may operate. If you are soliciting funds through your social media, website, or by sending solicitations to potential donors in other states, your organization will need to follow the laws of each state. Many states require a charitable organization to register, and some require fees and submission of an independent audit of your organization.[47]

The Financial Accounting Standards Board (FASB) updated its accounting standards, including those for nonprofits, in December 2017. These include disclosures regarding liquidity, expenses, and restricted vs. unrestricted funds. A CPA who is well-versed in nonprofit accounting can help you meet the FASB accounting standards for your organization.

Compliance not only applies to the requirements of government regulations, but it can also apply to requirements implemented by the board. All actions should be transparent and above board, and the only people who should benefit from the charity are those you serve in fulfilling your mission.

---

[46] ("Where can I find an organization's Form 990 or 990-PF?" [2022]) Candid.org Learning https://learning.candid.org/resources/knowledge-base/finding-990-990-pfs/

[47] ("Charitable Solicitation – Initial State Registration" [March 28, 2022]) IRS.gov https://www.irs.gov/charities-non-profits/charitable-organizations/charitable-solicitation-initial-state-registration

# CCSP

Connections Community Support Programs (CCSP), a Delaware nonprofit founded in 1985, was a multi-faceted health and human services organization. It had more than 100 locations throughout the state, employing over 1,100 people. They provided healthcare and treatment in many different capacities including psychiatric/behavioral health services, substance use disorder treatment, housing and veterans' services, intellectual disabilities services, and operation support services.

CCSP provided healthcare and behavioral healthcare in Delaware state prisons for a number of years until the contract was ended in 2020, and it was not re-awarded the $60 million contract. CCSP still held two state contracts with the Department of Health and Human Services and the Department of Services for Children, Youth, and Their Families.

In 2021 the U.S. Attorney's office filed two lawsuits against CCSP claiming the nonprofit made false claims to receive $4.5 million in improper payments and did not adequately document its narcotics distributions. The lawsuit claimed that for many years, CCSP was improperly billing government programs for mental health services and failing to properly monitor and document its controlled substances inventory.

The government's claims were based on a whistleblower suit filed by two former CCSP employees. The False Claims Act provided the whistleblowers with a share of the $13,757,520.60 judgement CCSP agreed to for the mental health service claims, as well as $1,621,571 to resolve the claims it violated the federal Controlled Substances Act by failing to keep accurate records.

In April 2021 CCSP filed for Chapter 11 bankruptcy after facing numerous lawsuits (including the judgements listed above) and tens of millions of dollars owed to companies that contracted with them. By October 2021 they had converted the Chapter 11 bankruptcy to a Chapter 7 proceeding.

The nonprofit is now defunct due to owing more than it could pay. It seems they thrived for years getting multi-million-dollar contracts from the state government and others, filing false claims, and not properly monitoring or documenting as required. They may not have had the infrastructure in place to do the variety of things needed for proper oversight. Eventually this all caught up to them and brought the once-successful organization down. To all who looked from the outside, CCSP seemed to be a very successful nonprofit. Looks can be deceiving.

## Travel & Reimbursement Policy

Implement a policy to reimburse volunteers for any out-of-pocket expenses they incur on behalf of your organization. Create a form to be submitted with receipts for items purchased on the charity's behalf. Make the policy clear to anyone who may incur expenses while planning events or doing other charity-related work. Spell out the types of expenses allowed, a maximum amount permitted without board or committee chair pre-approval, and who may incur these expenses on the nonprofit's behalf. Be clear that there will be no reimbursements without valid receipts. Consider whether reimbursement should be limited to pre-approved expenses only. The form should be readily available and easy to submit. (In many cases, volunteers will consider these expenses a donation to the charity and will not ask to be reimbursed. In this case, provide them with a tax receipt for their donation.)

Once you have hired employees, the policy should be extended to cover their expenses for travel and other expenses they may incur.

### Travel & Reimbursement Policy considerations:

- Form to fill out and submit with receipts and/or other documentation validating the claim should include:
  - Name of employee incurring expense(s)
  - Exact date(s) incurred
  - Item(s) they paid for (per diem allowance, meals, accommodation costs, travel expenses, program materials)
  - The specific business purpose generating the expense(s)
- Require expenses to be submitted within 60 days of incurring them
- If any expense funds are given to the employee up front, they should be required to return any funds not used for the specified purpose within 120 days, or the overage will be added to their wages on their W-2 and will be taxed as such
- Volunteers may deduct 14 cents per mile on their personal tax returns for all mileage on their personal vehicle directly related to volunteering for nonprofit organizations (they may add up mileage for all nonprofit organizations they are involved with – for meeting attendance, board business, volunteer activities, charitable events)

- The IRS allows reimbursement of 65.5 cents per mile[48] for nonprofit employees on official business, so the employer may reimburse up to that amount – any overage is considered wages and must be accounted for as such

## Fundraisers

Fundraising events can be small, intimate affairs or they can be hundreds of people gathered in a large hall. They should evolve and change as your nonprofit evolves. Your organization may consider having a few different types of fundraisers that appeal to different populations of attendees. Be sure your event can attract a sufficient number of attendees before incurring all of the expenses and volunteer hours required to organize and run a successful event.

In the past few years, crowdsourcing or crowdfunding has become a popular way to fundraise. These terms refer to any type of effort to raise money with donations from large numbers of people, usually online. There are a number of different platforms from which to choose. Do your research to find a reputable one that will enable you to actually collect the funds you work hard to obtain. Also remember that if you are crowdfunding, you will need to register in all the states where your outreach takes you.

## Planning a Fundraising Event

Even small fundraising events require a lot of time and planning to be successful, so the job should not be left to one or two individuals. A committee should be formed many months ahead to ensure enough planning time. In fact, about a month after the most recent fundraiser, the committee should meet for a wrap-up meeting, take note of what did and did not work, and start planning next year's event if it will be held again.

The event committee should already know from the annual budget how much they are attempting to raise and how much they may spend to do so. The treasurer or those paying for the event expenses should also be fully aware of the expense budget to quickly notice any red flags if the committee is getting out of control with spending. At first notice, they should bring this to the attention of the president and other board members.

---

[48] ("IRS issues standard mileage rates for 2023; business use increases 3 cents per mile" [December 29, 2022]) IRS.gov https://www.irs.gov/newsroom/irs-issues-standard-mileage-rates-for-2023-business-use-increases-3-cents-per-mile

Plan your date early, and check with other local nonprofits known for their annual events, so you are not in direct competition on the same date. If you need to rent an event space, lock it in as soon as you know details about the type of event, how many people you expect, and the date it will be held. Once locked in, publish your date on local event calendars.

If you plan on honoring or giving an award to someone, tell them early and confirm that they will be able to attend on the chosen date. (If not, the choice needs to be made to change the event date or to move on to the next person on the list of potential honorees.)

**Some items you should consider investing in are:**

- Step and repeat banner
    - Large sign used for a backdrop for photos at events and for brand advertisement
    - There are all types of retractable or telescoping signs available through most printers
    - Be sure your organization's logo is large enough to be seen and recognized, but also consider spreading the "repeat" out so it is not too busy
    - You can include the logos of event sponsors, but realize this makes your step and repeat obsolete after one event if the sponsors change
- Logo tablecloth(s) for check-in table and for booth tables at networking and other events
- Marketing materials (brochures, logo-branded handouts)
- Pipe and drape system to build a false wall or mask or divide off an area

**Other things that should be done as early as possible:**

1. Put together the **event committee**. Each event committee should have multiple members, and can include board and staff members as well as volunteers from outside the organization. The committee chair is usually a board member (especially before you have hired staff members), so they can report progress back to the board. The committees will vary depending on your event and your organization.

    **Event committees may include:**

    - **Overall Event Chair(s)**
    - **Sponsorship** – to recruit corporate and individual sponsors who will donate in exchange for advertisement in your event materials and at the event venue

- **Raffles/Auction** – to solicit raffle items and donors, package the items, and sell tickets before and at the event (be clear about what items you are looking for and what you will or will not allow); this **may require a permit** in your area, so the raffle chair(s) should obtain the permits if necessary

- **Liquor License** – if you will be serving alcohol at a venue that does not have its own liquor license, you will need to check into what is required in your area

- **PR/Communications** – press releases, social media posts, invitations to get the word out about the event

- **Venue Liaison** – to work out details and be sure there are no miscommunications

- **Registration** – responsible for processing all event registrations, creating attendance lists, name tags, and seating charts if there will be assigned seating

- **Awards** – securing the awardees (and ensuring they are available to attend on the specified date), choosing the awards, ordering them, and making sure the awards are printed correctly and arrive at the venue on time

- **Decorating/Entertainment** – choosing the colors and theme for the event, planning the decorations and purchasing or otherwise acquiring them, hiring and preparing the entertainment, decorating the space before the event

- **Finance** – responsible for all money matters the day of the event including having cash to make change if it will be needed, getting credit card swipers and training those who will be using them (and making sure there is wi-fi access to be able to use them), creating systems to account for the different categories of cash and credit card income that night (want to know raffles vs. day-of registration payments vs. day-of donations), two or more people who will count any cash before it leaves the venue, and a responsible person to take home the cash and receipts and make a deposit into the bank account as soon as possible

- **Coordinator for those you serve** – if they will be attending the event or speaking to the attendees, this committee will invite them and give them a way to sign up (if they do not need to pay to attend, they will register differently), prepare them for mingling with the other guests (networking tips) and/or for their speech

2. Call or email the offices of **local politicians** to try to get on their calendars to attend your event. Become friends with their schedulers and sell them on why their bosses should be interested in supporting your organization.

3. Plan **how your event tickets and raffle tickets will be sold**. Set up an online portal and beta test it before it goes live if you will be selling online.

4. If you will have an auction, you may want to sign up for online **auction software.**

5. Decide if your **invitation** will be mailed, emailed, or both. Find someone to design the print and/or email versions of the invitation. Be sure to include:

    ○ The theme/name of the event

    ○ Your logo

    ○ Type of event (tea party, cocktail party, dinner, luncheon, beef and beer, etc.) and what type of food and drinks will be provided (should they come hungry or already fed?)

    ○ Expected dress requirements (formal attire, cocktail, business, business casual, casual)

    ○ Date & time

    ○ Location

    ○ Awardees/Honorees

    ○ Raffle or auction items to entice (if applicable)

    ○ Event sponsors with their logos

    ○ A list of board, advisory council (AC), and event committee members (if there are some on the committee who are not on the board or AC) to entice their friends and admirers to attend

    ○ Contact information (email and/or phone number of someone in charge of the event) to report any problems with registration or to ask questions about the event – be sure to assign someone who is responsive in a timely fashion

    ○ How to register for the event

    ○ How to make a donation or buy raffle tickets if unable to attend

    These items may seem obvious, but I have seen invitations that have left off some pertinent information, and it caused more stress in an already stressful time.

6. If you plan to create a **video** that will be shown at the event, the videographer should be chosen at least six months prior to ensure enough time to schedule interviews with subjects, record the interviews, and edit to create the final product.

7. Sponsorships can bring in a lot of extra funding for an event. First decide what the sponsorship dollar levels will be, and create a sponsorship packet that explains what sponsors will receive for each level and why it may be worth their while to sponsor at a higher level. There are more details about **sponsorship packets** in Appendix VII.

8. **The sponsorship income goals should be part of the organization's annual budget.** Start reaching out to potential sponsors as early as possible because many companies decide on their sponsorships early in the year and have a spending limit.

9. There are good reasons to incorporate **awards or honors** into your fundraiser. If you are honoring a well-known person in the community, you may want to mail or email a "Save the Date" notice announcing it, so others are sure to block that date on their calendars. Honorees can really be a big draw to your event, and they can bring in new people who will learn about your organization. Their friends and family members will want to attend to honor them.

   A committee should bring a slate of possible awardee/honoree candidates to the board, event committee, or other event decision-makers months before the event. It is important to have a first, second, and third choice (this does not need to be public knowledge) if, for any reason, the first choice is not available on the date of your event or for some other reason.

   You may want to offer two or three awards for different categories relating to how people have helped your organization. One award could go to a graduate of your programs who has gone on to do great things. They may not be a huge draw to your event, but their story will speak volumes to those in attendance.

   Once the honorees are chosen, the award design should be planned, and the award plaques or trophies should be ordered. Do this well ahead of the event in case there are problems – the name is spelled incorrectly, the award arrives damaged, etc. Choose a very reliable person or people in your organization to make certain the awards arrive at the venue on time the day of the event.

10. The event chairs, coordinating with the committee chairs, should create a **"Run of Show"** document that breaks the event down by time. This should list every speaker, video, and other details, so all involved know what to expect and whether or not the event is running on time. Multiple copies of this should be brought to the event for use behind the scenes.

11. Include in the live event program a **tug-at-the-heartstrings story** about how your organization is helping people in your community. Invite one or two of your program graduates to speak, talking about their hard-fought journey and how your organization helped better their life. This is a good place to add a "special appeal" for donations.

12. Give each speaker a time limit and ensure they stick to it, so you do not lose audience interest and attention. Be sure to build in time to thank the board, advisory council, sponsors, donors, and event committee members.

13. You may also **create and print a program** for each guest. Include an event agenda, a succinct history of the organization and its great work in the community, the list of committee members responsible for putting together the event, the event sponsors, bios of honorees, etc.

As you plan the event, take good notes laying out how the different pieces were put together. If volunteers will be working at the registration table, selling raffle tickets, or doing other specific tasks, write up simple but clear instructions as to what is expected of them. After the wrap-up meeting, **put together instructions and a timeline for each piece of the event, so the people doing it the next time do not have to start from scratch.**

## Fundraising Campaign

A fundraising campaign consists of raising funds during a specified period of time with a goal of a certain predetermined dollar amount. This happens once or twice a year for many nonprofits. In addition to the dollar goal, the organization's secondary (or maybe primary) goal should be to raise awareness of the good work your organization is doing.

A request letter may go out by mail and/or email, and there can be additional campaign-related posts on your social media channels. Direct people to your website or a campaign page that shows off the programs you offer and the difference you are making.

If possible, include a hand-written note by a board member or staff person on the mailed letter, thanking them for their past support (if applicable) and hoping you can count on them this year. This is especially effective if the person writing the note has a connection to the potential donor, and if a bit of the note shows through a window on the envelope. The recipient is more likely to open the letter and read the contents if they recognize the personalization.

You may have attrition of more than 50% of donors each year, meaning those who gave in the past may not be able or interested this year. Always be adding people to your prospect list. Ask new board members for names, and be constantly thinking about who may be a good prospect. Network, Network, Network to meet new prospective supporters.

## Capital Campaign

As your nonprofit grows, there may come a time when you need to think about raising a large sum of money over a certain period of time (usually 12 to 24 months), which is known as a capital campaign (CC). The funds may be needed to acquire or renovate a building for program and office space or other development projects. The capital campaign can include creating a scholarship or endowment fund, or you may run a separate endowment campaign for this purpose.

A capital campaign should not be entered into lightly and should have known support behind it before the campaign starts. Below is a very simplified overview of a complicated process.

The first step is to determine the total amount needed for each of the items on your wish list. A realistic estimate of costs for building or renovations or other capital expenditures should be calculated by an architect or contractor. Make sure to include a reserve or endowment for upkeep of the new building. Next, an in-depth study should be implemented to determine if your current donors and others in the community would be open to funding these large projects in addition to or instead of funding the mission and operations.

**Look into hiring experienced campaign study consultants.** It is worth the cost up front to determine if there will be support before going to all of the time, trouble, and expense of starting a campaign. Many funders ask if you have taken the step of conducting an independent feasibility study prior to making a gift. Campaign consultants should report to a special committee within your organization that can answer questions and supply any needed materials to support the research process.

**Steps to take before launching a capital campaign:**

1. Make a **Case for Support** to present to potential stakeholders
   - A history of the organization and its accomplishments
   - Goals and impact summary
   - Details of what the intended capital campaign will support and why it is needed
   - Costs and architectural drawings or other specifics

2. **Conduct interviews** with people who have varied connections to the organization, including those who were involved in the early days, those currently involved, loyal donors who can be counted on every year, lapsed donors, and those in the community with wealth or influence who could help drive donations. Have trusted individuals from outside the organization set up one-on-one confidential interviews with stakeholders from many different facets of your organization to try to get balanced input and advice. Be sure to ask at the end of each interview if there is a level of giving they would be comfortable with from the giving tiers presented. This is not a commitment of dollars from them, but it can give an idea of the overall amount you may be able to raise when adding these figures together. Ask if they will be willing to help with the fundraising in some capacity. There will be a cap on the number of in-person interviews you can realistically accomplish.

3. **Send out a questionnaire** asking many of the same questions to the next tier of stakeholders. In this step you can reach a much larger group of people to get feedback.

4. **Compile the results** of the interviews and questionnaire responses, and present the findings to the board.

5. If the findings lean toward a community that is receptive to funding your capital projects, the board or the consultant team can **put together promotional materials and set a date to launch** the capital campaign.

6. **Set up committees** to manage the actual fundraising and to keep track of the campaign financing. Other committees include public relations, events, and how donors will be thanked and acknowledged.

7. Before the very public rollout, you will have the **quiet phase** of your campaign where you solicit top donors. The objective of this phase should be to raise more than half of the overall campaign goal.

8. The **public phase** should include a lot of **fanfare, press releases, and social media announcements** to get the word out and remind people of your organization's good work in the community and need for support for your capital campaign.

9. Now the work of following up on pledges, thanking donors and volunteers, and putting the dollars to work begins!

Once you commit to a capital campaign, form a plan to adjust the outcome if you are not able to raise all of the funds needed. Consider finding additional funding sources like grants or loans if needed.

# CHAPTER 9

# GRANTS & CONTRACTS

———— ·•●•· ————

*"When you do good work, good things come."*

Anya Lindsey-Jenkins
(Executive Director of Big Brothers
Big Sisters of Delaware)

As your nonprofit grows, you will be sewing together a patchwork of grants and other funding to cover your costs. You also need to pay attention to and keep track of any restrictions placed on the funds by each source. Funders tend to be cyclical in their foci, so today they may be intent on funding early childhood development, but in a couple years they may all switch to a focus on employment and training. It helps if your organization is multi-faceted and can continue to get funding in at least one area within these focus cycles. However, stay true to your mission, and do not add a focus area solely to try to get funding.

## Grants

Grants are sums of money given by an organization or the government for a particular purpose. Private or public foundations, other public charities, for-profit companies, or government entities are all sources for grants.

Just as there are many sources for grants, there are also varied structures and purposes donor organizations have for giving grants. Foundations are governed by their bylaws and missions and many are very focused in their giving criteria – education, underserved youth, arts & culture, environmental stewardship, social services, health & wellness, women's programs, or animal welfare are some of the purposes they may be bound by. Other granting public charities may have similar parameters.

Corporate grants are usually focused on helping the local community, and their foci may change as the community needs evolve. Government grants can come from all sectors of government, and the focus will depend on the government entity and those it intends to serve. There may be restrictions on applying. For example, the State of Delaware requires that a nonprofit have its 501(c)(3) status for at least two years before being allowed to apply for state funding.

There are various government grants available for all types of programs. **www. Grants.gov** provides a free, searchable database of all federal funding opportunities. The keywords for your search should be very specific to the work you do. You may also find government grants through your state, county, or local municipality.

Each grant will not only differ by its focus, but each will also have different timelines for application due dates, type of application and information required, and some grants are by invitation only. Certain grantors will have grant cycles once or twice a year where they hold a mandatory information meeting for anyone who intends on applying, then the application is open for a few weeks, after which they choose the recipients. Start by visiting a grantor's website to look at their specific requirements.

A nonprofit that is successful in getting grant funding usually has a continuous process of researching grant options and has an experienced grant writer. First, you need to be sure that any grant you are applying for is accepting applications at that time and that they don't require you to be invited to apply. This will save hours, sweat equity, and even printer ink and postage if not an online application.

### Making Good Connections

Mark* started a nonprofit in Louisville, Kentucky. It is an out-of-school program for at-risk kids. Beth*, the head of a family foundation, met him in 2015 in the lobby of a church when she was there for a community program. A mutual friend (a Louisville City Councilwoman) was very excited to introduce Mark to Beth so he could tell her about his new nonprofit. The family foundation Beth runs funds out-of-school programs, so she was interested to hear about his organization.

Beth said this type of introduction happens a lot, and it does not necessarily lead to a relationship between the two organizations. However, in this case it proved beneficial for both parties. That day she gave Mark her business card, and they kept in touch. Mark's organization was very early in its process with very little funds – he was not paying himself a salary and had a hard time paying the bills – but he was SO passionate about it.

Beth knew that he was not yet at the place where she could take a proposal to her board to fund his organization because there was not enough history, experience, or structure. Her board likes to fund up-and-comers, but this was still too soon.

Beth, as the Executive Director of the family foundation, has some discretionary funds that she can deploy without board approval. She keeps this pretty quiet and uses the funds for cases like this where she sees passion and progress. Beth does not give a lot of detail about this process to the recipients to prevent future nonprofits from knowing about and competing for her discretionary funds.

She started working with Mark, had him submit a formal proposal, and they reviewed it at the staff level instead of taking it before the board. The staff approved a $7,000 grant because they liked his program and wanted to see what he could do with the funds. That amount was about 20% of his overall budget at the time.

Mark used the funds well and reported back the great things his program had done with them. Because he had put the funds to good use and followed up with reports and data, they gave him an additional $7,000 the next year.

The family foundation gave Mark feedback on each proposal he submitted, and how he measured and reported on the program, to help him improve those skills for the next time. He took all of the feedback and applied it. Mark had been such a good student, the family foundation offered to pay to send him to a new leaders' academy program and to a conference at the local Center for Nonprofit Excellence.

The foundation started selectively introducing Mark to other local foundations that they knew would also be supportive of an organization in the early-stage roughness that was not yet polished and pretty. He started to make more and more connections.

Then, one day, the local community foundation "discovered" him. They wrote an article about how they had found this great new nonprofit leader. The reason they "found" him was because Beth's family foundation had been coaching and helping him, and he was doing a great job of accepting that help. He took the feedback, suggestions, and small grants, and put them to work to better his organization. His "luck" was actually him being READY when the opportunity presented itself in the form of the community foundation.

Finally, Mark's organization became established enough that the family foundation invited him to submit a formal proposal, and this time they took it before the board. They approved grants of $25,000 for each of the next two years. Just recently the board approved almost $70,000 for Mark's organization – ten times what they had given him at the start!

Through this relationship, Mark received coaching, community connections, and funding for his nonprofit. The family foundation found a willing student and, eventually, a successful and sustainable nonprofit that fit their funding parameters.

*The names have been changed for this story.

Start as soon as possible to build relationships with potential funders, long before you intend to ask them for a grant. The funder-nonprofit relationship can be a bit intimidating, especially for a leader of a new nonprofit, but it can turn out to be beneficial in many ways. Grantors are required to give money to programs that fit their parameters, so they are always looking to fund programs and find ways to help those programs be very effective. There is nothing adversarial or power-driven from most grantors. They want to be helpful, and you may find that they can help in other ways even if they are unable to award you a grant.

An open, honest, and close relationship with a funder could lead to help when your organization is not sure how to answer a particular question on another funder's application, or maybe they will find ways to fund your organization in times when things are not going well. Some foundations have a bit of seed money that is less than a single grant may be, but they do not have to go through the formal grant approval process to award these funds. The executive director may have the authority and autonomy to give small donations to those they believe in. Foundations may also have a lot of community clout, so if they believe in you, they may pass the word on to others.

Sometimes a check is not the best thing you can get from a funder. They may also have resources that can help you to better your organization. A funder may be able to help you "unstick" a problem or situation, or they may connect you with someone who has power or influence that you need. In some instances, these "donations" can be much more valuable than cash.

## Applying for Grants

Each grant you apply for will come with different requirements and instructions. The applications may ask similar questions, but each may require the answer to be given in a particular way. **There is nothing more important in being considered for a grant than following all of their instructions to the T, and submitting everything they ask for.** Funders are always looking for the data behind the ask, so provide as much data as you can to prove that your plan is credible, that there is a need for it, and be able to back it up with evidence you have gathered. You may not have your own program results yet, but you can track data collected by universities or other public institutions around the social problem you are trying to cure.

Most will want:

- The name, address, and other contact information for your organization
- An overview of your nonprofit and its mission
- Proof of 501(c)(3) status (IRS letter)
- Dollar amount you are requesting
- Program purpose, goals, and outline
- Who is the target population? How do you intend to find and recruit them?
- What is the need you expect to fill?
- Who will be served?
- How many individuals do you intend to serve with the program, and how much will it cost per individual? (If you are asking for $50,000 for a program that expects to directly affect 10 people, is it worth it, in the funder's view, to pay $5,000 per person?)
- Project timeline
- Methods for measuring success of the program
- How you will know the program has been a success
- Project budget and/or organization's overall budget (be sure to submit only the numbers they are requesting)
- Other funding sources and fundraising plans for this program in addition to this grant (be transparent about other grants you have applied for – you may or may not receive them)
- Who in your organization will be responsible for running the project

Grantors will look at the overall structure and soundness of your organization. They will look at the diversity of your board to see if it reflects the community you are serving. They want to know that your board believes in your mission and the organization, so they will look to see if there is 100% board participation in donating to the organization each fiscal year. (See more about this under "Board Formation" in Chapter 5.)

Funders want to invest in something your organization is uniquely positioned to do and is especially good at, so they can be a part of having a magnifying effect. They want proof of administrative excellence, that the nonprofit has an organizational purpose and goals, that board members understand their fiduciary duties, that the organization has enough operating funds in the bank to allow it to stay solvent through unexpected turbulence, and that it has expenses in line with its peers (with the majority of expenses going directly to mission programming). They may require proof of an independent audit. The funders have fiduciary duties, too – to fund projects and organizations that are doing what they said they would do if the grantor agrees to fund them.

The grant writer should make a clear business case for how your organization runs, what you plan to do with this program, and how you will measure its impact. Provide proof of past successes when giving the history of your organization.

Be sure to follow all rules, deadlines, and reporting requirements set by the grantor. The grant application should be specific to a program, and not just a general application for funding your whole organization or a menu of program options hoping the funder will choose the one that appeals most to them. They want to see a well-thought-out program that fits within their funding parameters. The program budget needs to make sense, with numbers that are logical and that are totaled correctly. It needs to justify the grant amount you are requesting. The application may ask what you could do if they only awarded partial funding and not the entire amount requested. Be honest about what you could do with $5,000 instead of $15,000. If you are not able to do this project without their funds, let them know that.

Your grants team should be constantly searching for new grant sources. Some foundations require you to wait a year or two before you can apply again, whether you received a grant or not. You may find a foundation that is willing to give you a substantial grant every year, but at some point, their circumstances may change. Funders want to know that you are applying elsewhere for grants, too, so they can rest assured that they are not your only source of funds and that they are investing in a sustainable program.

Grant writing is a science and an art. There is tremendous competition for most grants, so it is important that the person or people applying for grants on your behalf have been properly trained in this area to give your organization the best chance at beating the competition. They will need to understand the nuances of the application requirements, fully understand your organization and its mission and focus, and be very clear in the sharing of that information.

You may be fortunate to find experienced grant writers who will volunteer their time. If not, consider paying for grant training for someone within your organization. Look for someone who is already a good writer, who has a passion for the mission.

There are grant writers who may be hired as independent contractors. They may work for an hourly rate, by the application, on retainer, or based on the average number and size of grants per month. Paying a grant writer a percentage of the grant money they are able to acquire is an unethical practice and should not be done. As with any contractor, you should have a clear contract to spell out the details of what is expected by both parties. Your local nonprofit support organization or grant writers association can help with this process.

When you are fortunate enough to receive a grant, be sure to keep in contact with the grantor, and continue to build your relationship with them. Invite them to send volunteers for specific projects so they can see firsthand the good you are doing with their funds.

Grantors want to hear how the funded program is going, whether the news is good or bad. Sometimes circumstances beyond your control have altered your program, and you may be a bit nervous to tell the funder you will not be able to use their funds in the way intended. Give them the courtesy of telling them what happened. It may be that they ask for a refund, or they may approve use of the funds for the pivot-project that you are doing instead. Most times they are very willing to work with you, especially if you have developed a good relationship with them. Do not use the funds for a different purpose than stated on your grant application without pre-approval of the change!

Always turn in, before the deadline, the required follow-up forms reporting on how the funds were used. If you want a chance to receive another grant from them in the future, this is a must. Funders want to know that your organization is run well enough to follow instructions and meet deadlines. They also want to feel that you are appreciative of their generosity.

## Combined Federal Campaign

Through OPM.gov (the Office of Personnel Management), nonprofits can apply to receive funds from the Combined Federal Campaign (CFC). It is similar to the United Way for federal employees who may opt to give a portion of each paycheck to the nonprofit of their choice. If a nonprofit has provided services in 15 or more different states or a foreign country within the three-year period preceding its application year, it may apply for the national CFC listing.

Those that do not meet the above criterion may be eligible to participate in the local section of the CFC Charity List. To be eligible for the local section, you must have provided services in the previous calendar year in the local CFC zone to which you are applying. You must submit financial statements including a 990 and a recent audit, and you must pay an application fee. It may be worth it to then have a dependable income stream going forward, and this process may get your name and mission out to those who would not otherwise know about you.[49]

## Government Contracts

Governments at all levels depend on charitable nonprofits to provide services to residents that would be more costly if provided by others. The nonprofit sector, as a whole, earns about a third of its total revenue by providing services under written agreements with governments.[50] In some cases the U.S. government disburses money to states and local governments for them to award grants using their local knowledge.

When your organization is ready to take on a government contract to expand its programming, you can search online and check with your peers in the industry. Look into the government agency that best matches your niche area. If you are in the environmental space, look at the Environmental Protection Agency (EPA). If you are in health and wellness, look at the Department of Health and Human Services (DHHS). There will be at least one government agency that covers the area of your mission both nationally and at the state or local level.

Nonprofits that are awarded federal funds are subject to myriad regulatory compliance requirements. Government agencies will audit and investigate grantees

---

[49] ("Learn Everything You Need to Know to Apply to the CFC Campaign" [2022]) Certified Federal Campaign https://cfccharities.opm.gov/app/#!/home

[50] ("Government Grants/Contracting [2022]) National Council of Nonprofits (Reprinted with permission from the National Council of Nonprofits.) https://www.councilofnonprofits.org/trends-policy-issues/government-grants-contracting

and contractors, and, if the receiving nonprofit has not complied with all stipulations, it may have to repay some of the funds or could face civil or criminal penalties. The National Council of Nonprofits spells out the rights nonprofits have under the new OMB (Office of Management and Budget) Uniform Guidance.[51]

Some organizations may find government contracts to be too restrictive. Also, a government contract may pay about 75% of the costs of your program in year one. The downside of government contracts is that, typically, they do not adjust for inflation. If you continue to receive the same contract year after year, eventually it may only be paying about 40-50% of your costs as those costs rise over time.

Receiving grants or government contracts will take your charity to the next level. You are no longer dependent on just the goodwill of individuals. Things will start to evolve...

---

[51] ("Nonprofits and the New OMB Uniform Guidance: Know Your Rights...and How to Protect Them" [2023]) National Council of Nonprofits (Reprinted with permission from the National Council of Nonprofits.) https:// www.councilofnonprofits.org/trends-and-policy-issues/federal-policy-tax-law/omb-uniform-guidance/ nonprofits-and-new-omb-uniform

CHAPTER 10

# EVOLVING/SUSTAINABILITY

———— ··•·· ————

*"New business models are altering workplaces*
*everywhere, in for-profit and nonprofit sectors alike.*
*Enterprises must constantly evaluate and change their*
*business models to survive."*

Timothy Clark (Author of *Business Model You*)

As your organization grows, the skillsets needed to run it will change. This involves walking a fine line between being adaptable to those changes, but also staying true to and grounded in your mission. It is important to not lose focus, whether you are a new organization or are celebrating 25 years of existence.

You may have planned all along to scale up your organization, programs, and staffing, but it is also perfectly fine to plan to remain a small, grassroots organization. Do what is best for your nonprofit and the community you are serving. The biggest challenge will be to remain relevant to the people you serve, volunteers, community leaders, and funders, far into the future.

Set aside the "organizational ego." Focus less on making the entity successful and more on how to meet the needs in the community (following your mission) in creative ways and with passion. This outward focus will ultimately help your organization remain sustainable and be successful.

If your nonprofit does not have ongoing programming (it is a granting organization that raises funds for others to do the programming), it may be easier to remain an all-volunteer organization for a longer period of time. If you provide programming, you will want to hire employees to lead the programs, apply for grants, and/or coordinate your volunteers. Having only volunteers is great in that it does not increase your overhead costs, but you will find that it is hard to count solely on volunteers because they have jobs and lives, and those things come before their charitable efforts. There is much more reliability and accountability with paid staff members.

When looking to start hiring, look first for people who are passionate about the mission and who fit into your organization's culture. Because you are running a business, it "pays" to have employees who are experienced business people. You need to have a strong and motivated TEAM of people in the "right seats" who know how to work independently and with the other employees and volunteers.[52]

Once you are at the point of hiring staff or seeking out grants, this changes the game, and catapults you into the business realm. You will need to balance what you pay in salaries with managing your bottom line. It is important to pay staff members a living wage and what they are worth, but if you overpay them, your potential funders will notice. This could prevent you from getting much-needed grants or other funding.

---

### Diversity Matters

Pamela* served on a board that did a search for a new executive director (ED) – four times in two years! The first three hires lasted only a few months each, but when I was speaking to Pamela in spring 2022, the fourth hire was about to celebrate one year with the organization.

For the first three rounds, the hiring committee did not have a diverse slate of candidates from which to choose. Pamela joined the committee when looking for the fourth candidate because of her background in HR. She screened resumes and conducted interviews, and she presented a diverse cross-section of candidates to the team – male, female, differing backgrounds, and a range of career experience. Prior to this last round, they had not considered one candidate who looked like the community the organization serves, and those candidates who rose to the top in the prior rounds did not work out – three times!

The board Pamela serves on has the motto: "We're not saviors," meaning WE are not saving THEM. Instead, they see themselves as the allies of the people they are supporting in the community. The current ED is more reflective of the community they serve, which makes the organization more successful overall.

* The name has been changed for this story.

---

[52] Collins, Jim *Good to Great and the Social Sectors: A Monograph to Accompany Good to Great* 2005

## Hiring

When it is time to start hiring employees, first congratulate yourselves for growing your nonprofit to this point! As soon as you finish doing that, start thinking about raising funds to pay for the new hires. This will take your budget to a whole new stratosphere – but the growth and reliable help should also take your funding options to the next level.

You may want to consider an equality-based staff rather than a hierarchical one, so each employee has authority to make decisions at the ground level for their program or area, but they are also accountable to the whole team for the overall goals and accomplishments. In this type of organization, there may be an executive director (or someone with a more equality-based title) who is responsible for the overall coordination, but who does not make ten times or even four times the salary of the other staff members. If they have a bit more responsibility, they may earn a bit more in salary.

The relationship between the board and the staff can be great or it can become toxic. There are some practices you can implement from the beginning, or add in later as they become necessary, to keep that relationship positive.

## Hiring an Executive Director

Your first hire may be an office manager who works on administrative tasks and coordinates volunteers. As you grow and have multiple offices or programs, you will need to hire an executive director (ED) who coordinates all of it. The ED will also be looking at longer-term planning and overseeing the budget for the whole organization.

Be sure that all involved understand the executive director's role is to execute the decisions and directives of the board, but they make no major decisions without the board's approval. They run and have oversight for the day-to-day operations, but ultimately report to and are accountable to the board. The board hires the executive director, has oversight for them, and may fire that person if they are not carrying out the board's directives satisfactorily.

The board should be careful to give the executive director room to work toward the mission. If the focus becomes too narrow and the board is too strict, the ED will only focus on the bottom line and will not have the time or energy to focus on the bigger picture. The board needs to support "mission over making money" and make that heard and understood throughout the organization.

The organization needs to make the communications and reporting channels clear to all. Employees should go directly to their supervisor with issues and not directly to board members. If you have an equality-based staff, there should still be a clear path to report problems and get assistance. Going to the board should be a last resort if staff members find they are not able to get results within the chain of command. The executive director should be made aware of all staff issues and should be the one to bring those issues to the board.

An executive director needs to understand "the numbers." This includes knowing how to read and understand budgets, balance sheets, profit & loss (P & L) statements, and financial projections. Of course, you will also want to look for other skillsets like HR knowledge; fundraising; how to create and evaluate programming; relationship building with government, donors, employees, and volunteers, etc. Depending on your budget, you may need to forego experience and hire a young graduate with a degree in a nonprofit-related field who you believe can learn some of the skills on the job.

Once your organization is experiencing growth and success, a lot of that success may be attributed to the leadership. Other organizations may try to hire them away from you, so you need to be ready for that possibility. You may need to counter-offer to try to keep them, and you will need to replace them if they choose to leave. Keeping your employees happy to work at your organization by offering competitive salaries and benefits along with a healthy work environment may make this a moot point.

## Additional Hired Assistance

Your early hires may be independent contractors or part-time employees you can count on to do the work and fill the gaps where your volunteers do not have expertise or just don't have the time to get to. These may include **office management** (day-to-day management, connecting and interfacing with the community and other partners, IT, thank-you letters to donors), a **business manager** (accounting and human resources [HR] functions), and **IT** assistance (help with daily computer functions or to maintain the website). You will quickly come to realize that a lot of the skills needed to successfully run your nonprofit are professional skills, so you should not try to "make do" with non-skilled volunteers or workers.

It is important to determine whether the individuals who are providing services are considered employees or independent contractors. If they are employees, you must withhold and pay income taxes, social security taxes, and Medicare taxes. You will also need to pay unemployment taxes on wages paid to the employees. The IRS has a 20-Factor Test to determine whether an individual can be considered an independent contractor, and therefore you would not be responsible for all of the withholdings.[53] Failure to withhold taxes when required can subject the organization, and potentially its directors, to significant liability.

When planning to hire a new employee, the board (and eventually the executive director) should put together a detailed job description that includes the skills requirements and the specific job functions the new employee will be required to do. Determine the number of days and hours per week this person will work, but know that this detail may be negotiated when you find the right candidate.

Be as detailed as possible about your must-haves, your would-like-to-haves, and your would-be-great-add-ons before posting your job. Think about who you already know who has these skills and may be interested, but be extra careful in considering hiring relatives or close friends of board or other staff members. Refer to your nepotism policy to see what is allowed. Think about the scenario where the employee does not work out for some reason and how that would play out. It is best to avoid even the appearance of a conflict of interest, so this is another reason to hire qualified candidates with an arms-length distance from board or staff members.

You may also want to look into paid or unpaid interns. Internship is a two-way street where you get inexpensive or free help, and they are learning the ins and outs of how to run a nonprofit or a program. They will gain valuable experience and will be adding to their resumé. Although you are not paying this person, it can create a lot more work for the person in your organization responsible for the intern's supervision, so it may take them away from the job you hired them to do.

Create compensation and HR policies (things like paid time off [PTO], paid leave, and onboarding and training) before your first hire. Look at what similar organizations are doing right and what they are doing wrong to create the policies that will work best for your organization. Of course, these can be amended as you grow and need to adjust. You can find salary ranges for most job titles/descriptions in your region online at websites like www.glassdoor.com, www.payscale.com, or www.keela.co/blog/nonprofit-resources.

Even if you are not able to pay your employees well, if you want to avoid high turnover, you will need to pay them fairly and treat them well in other ways. Offer them things like an employer-sponsored retirement plan, health insurance, paid

---

[53] ("Independent Contractor (Self-Employed) or Employee?" [May 2022]) IRS.gov https://www.irs.gov/businesses/small-businesses-self-employed/independent-contractor-self-employed-or-employee

vacation time, and even small treats like a staff lunch once a month. These will cost your organization more than if you did not offer them, but it will end up costing a lot more when disgruntled, underpaid, and underappreciated employees turn over at a high rate, and you have to continuously search for, interview, and train new employees.

You may want to outsource some of the operations functions to cut down on your staffing needs. There are many companies that specialize in managing HR and/ or payroll and benefits for small organizations, or you may outsource things like accounting or bookkeeping. This way you have more time and energy to focus on your mission. Do an online search to find the company that best serves your needs, and be sure to get references before hiring them.

When your organization moves from an all-volunteer operation where the board has gotten used to being a "working" board responsible for accomplishing the day-to-day tasks, it may be a difficult transition when turning the operations over to the executive director and staff members. It is important for the long-term success and growth of the organization that the board adjusts and moves to the role of oversight. They should no longer be involved in the daily tasks.

## Over-Stressing the System

Sarah worked for a large social service agency. There was so much pressure at the executive level to "make the bottom line" and to keep up the organization's reputation that the individual needs of the staff and the programs were ignored.

The top executive was running so many programs and was under so much pressure that she could not or did not take the time to care that one (or more) of the programs was too understaffed or under-funded to be able to fulfill the contract (funding) goals properly. The staff members could see that they did not have enough staff or enough paid hours to complete the contract. The executive just insisted the staff needed to work harder.

The ultimate result was that the contract that was meant to "do good" for people was not being done well – not because the organization didn't care, but because the goals were not obtainable with the resources they had. The nonprofit was still paid for the contract, but they were over-stretched, so the funder of the contract was not getting what they should have gotten, and the clients were not being well served.

The organization should have looked at the resources available for the program before signing the contract and committing to it. They did not have funds to hire more staff to accomplish the stated goals. Those at the top only thought about how the contract made their nonprofit look good to others. It was the popular program to do at the time, but they did not plan for how they could fulfill it. In the end, they were doing a disservice to the people on the receiving end of the program as well as over-working and over-stressing their staff.

Eventually, Sarah and others left. They had seen these situations play out over and over, and they did not have hope for a better outcome in the future. The nonprofit lost good employees which only exacerbated the lack of resources needed to accomplish the goals.

The hierarchical structure in an organization can lead to a failure like the one Sarah lived through. The staff members (boots on the ground) may tell the ED it is not possible to complete the work with the existing resources. The ED then reports this to the board. The board is all-volunteer, and they only meet at certain times, so the ED has to wait to present it to them. The board discusses the matter and may not come to a decision about it until the next board meeting. This lag time in decision-making can add to the initial problems. The board should work to find ways to eliminate overly burdensome procedures that could cause failures in the system. They may want to consider creating fast-track options for decisions that cannot or should not be put on hold.

## Endowment

As your organization finds success in serving its mission as well as procuring funding, you may want to start investing in an endowment fund. This is a long-term investment in your future. In the short term, you will be paying into the endowment with no return. It could be an annual investment to transfer a certain percentage of your revenue, or it could be that in more bountiful years you invest what you feel you can spare, and in leaner years you abstain.

In most instances, the principal you have paid in to an endowment cannot be touched to allow the fund to grow over time, but once you have built up tens of thousands of dollars, the interest from the fund may be withdrawn annually in perpetuity, and this amount will increase as the core balance and/or the interest rate increases. The annual endowment withdrawal (typically 4-6% of the total amount of the fund) will be a welcome addition to the income portion of your financials, as it will be automatic funds that you do not have to find or apply for.

If your organization has plans to be around for a long time, starting an endowment sooner rather than later makes sense because eventually it will pay out to your nonprofit far more than you have paid in to it. Check with your local community foundation or nonprofit advisor to find the right fit for your organization.

## Partnering

Logan Herring, CEO of the WRK Group[54] nonprofit in Wilmington, Delaware says they thrive on partnering with organizations that can help them provide support to those they serve. They have a "Thanksgiving Day Model" where everyone is invited to bring their best dish to the table. WRK Group does not pretend to be able to cook the entire meal themselves. When everyone contributes, there are plenty of leftovers.

Logan says that many times nonprofits are afraid to share or work together because they fear that "food on your plate is no food on my plate." His organization believes in "an abundance theory, not a scarcity mentality." When all work together, there is plenty to go around.

Consider where your gaps in knowledge, workforce, or support may be, and look for other organizations you may partner with to be able to offer a more well-rounded service. This could cut down on duplicate services in your region, or could fill in where services did not exist previously.

## Learning

Your organization leaders should commit to becoming lifelong learners. Things in the world are constantly changing, and people are always inventing new and better ways to accomplish their goals.

Colleges, universities, nonprofit support organizations, community foundations, and other groups offer an array of nonprofit and business courses. They range from online webinars to certificate programs to undergraduate or graduate degrees. Take

---

[54] The WRK (pronounced "work") Group is comprised of three aligned organizations and more than 200 employees who share a collective mission to empower the community to reach its full potential by eliminating the barriers of structural racism and revolutionizing teen engagement. https://wrkgroup.org/

advantage of courses in leadership, grant writing, fundraising, board excellence, succession planning, or other nonprofit best practices.

Learning does not have to be a formal process. Those at the top of your organization should have an open line of communication with other staff members and with people in the community. Lower-level staff members are the "boots on the ground" who are in the trenches and know what is going on in the community. Consistently reaching out to members of the community or giving them easy access to reach out to you may help keep you informed as to changes or problems in the local area. This could help you effectively navigate around any barriers there may be to delivering your programs.

## Evaluation

On an annual basis, the board should do an **assessment of staff, programming, and other important parts** of the organization, as well as a **board self-assessment**. The objective of this process is to help you determine if you are meeting your goals and making progress in advancing your mission. This should also be a time when you make sure your goals and programs are still aligned with your mission. Additionally, you may want to look at whether your industry or your community is changing, and how you can adjust to meet these changes.

The board may come to the conclusion that the existing **mission and vision statements** are no longer relevant to the type of work you are doing to answer the needs in the community. They may need to dig deep to determine how these statements should be changed, updated, and enhanced so they accurately reflect the Value Proposition of the organization.

All supervisors should use an **employee evaluation** form to honestly review each direct report's performance. They should share the evaluations with an HR committee of the board and go over them with the individual staff members, giving valuable feedback. The board should do the same to evaluate the executive director's strengths and weaknesses. Expectations should be made clear during the hiring process and should be re-emphasized in the evaluation process.

There may be employees who have been with the organization for a number of years who show up to work every day, and who may be considered loyal employees. But loyalty does not always equate to service. Take an honest look at whether each employee is adding value and fits within your evolving framework. Are there some who show up each day because they have settled into an easy job where not much is expected of them? It is all right to let "loyal" members go if they no longer fulfill a need or do not seem to be adding value in working toward your mission.

Firing an employee who is underperforming must be preceded by conversations with these employees, documentation of the problems and conversations, and performance improvement plans to give them an opportunity to rectify the problems. You may want to seek legal counsel to ensure you are protecting the organization if you choose to terminate.

## Board Self-Assessment

When the board self-assesses, they also need to assess whether each board member is pulling their weight. If there are members who are not, have a frank discussion with them and, if they are not willing or able to change their behavior to become a valued member of the team, the rest of the board should not hesitate to let them go. They may be of better service to the organization as an Advisory Council member or volunteer for a specific short-term project. Board members should be honest with themselves and the rest of the board when they are no longer able to commit 100% to being a great board member. Something may have happened in their lives that compromises their ability to fulfill their obligation to the organization such as illness, work or family matters, or they may have become less captivated by the organization or cause, and they should be willing to step down to make room for someone who is ready and able.

Board assessments should also ensure that all are working toward the same mission and goals, and that the organization itself is still relevant and necessary. There may come a time when this is no longer the case, and the board needs to face that truth and determine next steps.

## SWOT Analyses

At regular intervals, you may want to perform a SWOT (strengths, weaknesses, opportunities, threats) analysis. First, determine what part(s) of your organization you would like to analyze. It could be a campaign, a program, or your marketing or other strategy. List all of the strengths you have. Then, do not be afraid to really look at the weaknesses that may impact your ability to compete. Next, look at opportunities that may help you grow if you take advantage of them. Lastly, seriously look at any threats like changes to laws, economic downturns, or other external factors that may negatively affect your organization.

SWOT analysis can help you with goal setting or strategic planning or to determine what went right or wrong and why. This may be done as part of an annual retreat meeting or other regularly scheduled strategic planning meeting. Be sure to seek out many different perspectives and take your time to really analyze your program or organization.

## Enterprise Risk Management

Enterprise Risk Management (ERM) provides a framework for determining an organization's most critical risks, and developing plans to manage and mitigate risk events having a significant impact on their financial and operational performance.[55] With ERM you are looking specifically at risks throughout your whole organization in many different areas – financial, board members, IT, governance, etc. Where SWOT is a tool for assessing capabilities, risk management is a tool for assessing the likelihood of success.[56]

## Founder Succession Plan

There was information about general succession planning in Chapters 5 and 7. Here we are looking at gracefully replacing the founder as the organization grows and flourishes. As your nonprofit evolves, it is very important that the historical knowledge and daily activity knowledge not be lost. The founder of the organization needs to have their story written so others in the future will know the origin. Maybe consider a video interview with the founder and some of the original board members, and keep copies of it in several locations so it is never lost.

The organization's founder has so much invested in the organization, it may be difficult for them to step back and let go. This is such a ubiquitous problem, the term **"Founder's Syndrome"** has become quite well-known. It is used to describe the founder's resistance to change and the problems that may arise from it. The founder needs to understand that as soon as the nonprofit is formed, it is an entity unto itself. The board governs the entity and makes all of the decisions concerning it. This includes deciding on the founder's role and when to replace them.

The energy needed to start up the organization is different from the energy needed to grow it, so the founder and the board need to recognize when change is necessary for growth. The organization should plan to keep the essence – the vision, mission, and values – in place when creating the succession plan. Having a passion for the mission means planning for its future.

---

[55] ("Getting Started with Enterprise Risk Management: A Guide for Nonprofits" by Amy Wares) https://erm.ncsu.edu/az/erm/i/chan/library/Getting_Started_with_ERM_-_A_Guide_for_Nonprofits.pdf

[56] ("SWOT vs. Risk Management" [February 15, 2010]) Reflections on Software Engineering by Michael Keeling https://www.neverletdown.net/2010/02/swot-vs-risk-management.html#:~:text=SWOT%20is%20a%20tool%20for.up%20with%20an%20overall%20strategy.

A succession plan for turning over the organization from the founder to the next generation of leaders should be developed early and adapted as the organization changes. This should involve grooming passionate board members and volunteers to be ready to take over leading the organization. If something unexpected happens to the founder before the planned succession time has arrived, these people will be able to adapt and carry on.

Rather than having one leader who is the only face of the organization, start to groom others to be spokespeople or to give speeches on behalf of the organization, so the public comes to recognize them as reliable members of the organization. The leader(s) may also want to start sharing their contact lists to enable others in the organization to develop relationships with funders.

If there is an untimely loss of the founder or leader, have a predetermined plan that designates a new temporary leader. There may be shock (or even grief if the loss is due to an unexpected death), but if your organization is able to quickly adapt to new leadership, you can at least start to make decisions from there. Of course, this plan will be different if the nonprofit is all-volunteer, if it has just a couple of employees, or if it is a larger organization with many employees. This, like most plans and strategies, should be revisited at regular intervals as the organization grows and changes.

It is never too early for the leader to put together a list of who to call in the first days and then in the first weeks if something happens to them. Others should know where and how to find all of the important information to run the nonprofit. Start to create a comprehensive database of the people important to the organization. This should include their donation details, but also information about their likes and their connections in the community, so that information is not lost with the absence of one person. Lastly, the leader should create a list of what it is they do day-to-day and month-to-month so items do not fall through the cracks if they leave suddenly.

In the best-case scenario, the founder will plan for an end date, and the new leader(s) will have time to learn and plan for that day. Because the process of the founder sharing their institutional knowledge may be time consuming, the board should consider offering the founder paid time to accomplish this during the turnover process.

Many churches require that once a leader steps down, that person will not have contact with parishioners for two years. This avoids people "taking sides" and continuing to show their loyalty to the former leader. It also gives the successor a chance to succeed without the former leader intervening.

## Rebranding

As your organization grows, changes, and morphs into something different from the early startup days, you may want to look at rebranding. Think about how you want to be perceived publicly and whether your current logo, tagline, and other outward-facing parts of your organization still work to promote the image you wish to project. If not, consider hiring a marketing and communications agency to help.

A good, full-service agency will gather information about what your organization does, how you see yourselves, and the public image you wish to project. Most importantly, your public image needs to reflect and magnify your mission. The agency will combine all of that to create a new and improved logo and tagline and help you incorporate your new image into all you do.

Be aware that the process of rebranding comes with costs you need to consider before going through with it. In addition to what the agency charges, you will need to update your website, letterhead, envelopes, volunteer T-shirts or aprons, building signage, etc. Take an inventory of what will need to be changed and weigh the costs of doing so before taking the plunge. You may also consider doing some advertising. You want the community to be familiar with the new image so you are findable and recognizable.

## Adding a New Appendage

There may come a time in your organization's life that you will want to or need to consider spinning off a section of the nonprofit. This could happen if the organization has a reason to become more politically involved than allowed within 501(c)(3) status, if you choose to add a social enterprise arm to your organization, or it could be that you have a program-related reason to sell items.

Some nonprofits operate with both a 501(c)(3) and a **501(c)(4)** corporation. The 501(c)(3) can raise tax-exempt funds to use toward helping those in the community and the organization's mission. The 501(c)(4) may endorse particular political candidates in an upcoming election who understand and will advocate for the mission of the tax-exempt arm. The (c)(4) is also allowed to raise money for the person-to-person work of engaging voters. You must notify the IRS within 60 days of formation of a (c)(4) by filing Form 8976 online. A 501(c)(4) is also exempt from federal taxes, but donations are not tax-deductible for those making donations.

Of course, the two entities will need to be separate corporations each with its own governance structure and IRS status, and the accounting will need to be completely separate. You may want to seek out the advice of a CPA and an attorney who have experience in advising on these two types of separate but joined entities.

When a nonprofit has substantial growth in its income-generating business activities that are not directly mission-related, these activities can trigger the **Unrelated Business Income Tax (UBIT)**.[57] The growth in this business activity may lead your organization to form a partnership with another existing entity or form a new independent **for-profit organization**.[58]

The income generated by these activities could put the tax-exempt status in jeopardy, so creating a separate entity can protect that status, can allow for more income generation, and it can also limit the liability of the nonprofit. For-profit affiliates can also offer equity ownership that a nonprofit cannot, so they may be able to attract outside investors, talent, and experienced employees.[59] There is no reason to be afraid to earn money that can offset the gaps in your nonprofit's funding. Just be sure to pay any owed taxes on that income.

Many times, a science-based nonprofit wants to **sell a part or invention** in conjunction with the services they offer, so this may be the right alternative to take advantage of the sales opportunities. Operating **a for-profit corporation** will require a full staff, completely independent of the nonprofit's staff, to run it. You should consult a knowledgeable attorney and/or CPA to discuss whether the corporation formed should be a C corporation, benefit corporation, social purpose corporation, LLC, or other form, and the benefits and risks of each option.

The nonprofit arm can receive donations, serve the mission, and educate the community. The business arm can sell the technology or other product and can raise money from venture capitalists, which a nonprofit may not do.

You may find the people your nonprofit serves could benefit from **job training or certification courses**. Finding a way to offer training and/or certifications to help those you serve could also help the surrounding community by increasing the number of qualified trained or certified employees for the local economy. Ask the businesses in your area what their needs are, rather than making bad assumptions. You may

---

[57] ("Unrelated Business Income Tax" [updated February 27, 2023]) IRS.gov https://www.irs.gov/charities-non-profits/unrelated-business-income-tax

[58] There are for-profit corporations that add a nonprofit arm to help fund charitable projects, but for this section, we are only discussing the nonprofit adding a for-profit arm.

[59] ("Forming a For-Profit Subsidiary of a Nonprofit" [2022]) The Law Office of Jeremy Chen http://jeremychenlaw.com/for-profit-subsidiary-of-a-nonprofit/

also find a way to train employees to run a for-profit arm of your organization that generates revenue for your mission.

A **social enterprise** is an organization or initiative that mirrors the social mission of a nonprofit (or government program) with the market-driven approach of a business. It is not a separate legal structure like a nonprofit or for-profit organization. The three most common business models of social enterprise organizations are Product organizations, Service organizations, and Marketplace organizations.

A Product organization produces a tangible product that addresses a gap in the local market and can be sold directly to members of the community or to other local businesses. Service organizations provide a service such as education, healthcare, or financial resources to their communities. These services can be sold directly to individuals or businesses in the community. Marketplace organizations match producers of products or services with buyers of the product or service. Access to the marketplace is usually free for the buyer, but the producer will pay a fee for each product sold.[60]

A social enterprise can be used to supplement traditional nonprofit funding sources like grants and donations. Your organization should do a full analysis of whether or not branching out in this way would be beneficial and an additional burden you are willing and able to take on. Look at the costs and benefits, the expertise needed to be successful, and whether this venture would dilute your organization's programmatic mission work. Check with a nonprofit attorney and CPA for guidance on successfully running a social enterprise while not putting your 501(c)(3) status in jeopardy.

Talk to your lawyers, accountants, and/or financial advisors to make sure you can do any of the above in a way that is legal, does not jeopardize your 501(c)(3) status, and mitigates your organization's risks. Also be sure to spell out in contract form how all involved parties can separate from the new venture if and when that time comes.

Every organization these days needs to have a public presence. Next, we will look at the "outward face" of the organization.

---

[60] ("Thinking of Starting a Social Enterprise? Here are 4 Things You Need to Know" by Thomas Rinaldi [June 26, 2019]) GlobalGiving https://www.globalgiving.org/learn/social-enterprise-nonprofit-tips

# CHAPTER 11

# COMMUNICATIONS

————— · • ● · —————

*"Tools are only as good as the people who use them."*

Bonnie Adler (Data Privacy & Security Expert)

There are many ways for your organization to interact with the rest of the world. The more you interact, the more people will become familiar with and passionate about your cause. The more passionate people, the more funding and volunteer efforts will come your way.

It is best to have an overall communications strategy led by one person who has an aerial view of all of the following: website, database, email outreach, giving platform, and social media. When you are just starting out, each segment may be overseen by a committee chair, with all of the segment chairs reporting to a communications chair.

## Be Findable!

The first way to start getting more recognition is to get acquainted with your local elected officials, community leaders, and other well-known people in the business and government arena in your area. These are the people with all the connections, and they may also help you find funding sources.

Part of your public outreach should be sending out **press releases** to local media outlets. (Do an online search to find sample press releases.) This should happen whenever your organization does something noteworthy. Include a profile for each new person when adding new board, advisory council, or staff members. If you will be honoring a well-known member of the community at your upcoming event, this is a good way to advertise your event at the same time you honor that person in the local media. If your organization was recognized for an award, put out a press release so everyone can read about the good work you are doing. When you receive a grant from a foundation, include the name of the foundation, express your gratitude, and include details about the great program they have funded. Share the published articles on your social media channels and your website to double the exposure.

Some may say press releases are a thing of the past, but they can still be a valuable component of your overall marketing and outreach plan. You can include videos and links to additional resources your nonprofit offers. Use a high-quality photo of the event or people, or your logo if you don't have a photo, to attract more attention. If you use often-searched keywords and phrases, it can help drive search engine optimization (SEO) traffic to the article and your website. Send the press releases to local business news outlets, nonprofit communications, and community foundations to publish. At the end of every press release, be sure to include your website or other ways for people to reach out to you.

Popular online sites people visit to look up details about a nonprofit are **Guidestar. org** and **CharityNavigator.org**. Part of being a transparent organization is listing all of your public and financial details including your 990. (Charity Navigator gives nonprofits a higher rating if they share their 990 and financial statements.) This will help potential donors see how much of your budget is going to administrative and fundraising expenses and how much goes directly to your mission.

Providing your nonprofit details on GuideStar could also make you eligible for grants without needing to fill out a grant application. There are organizations tasked with giving funds to nonprofits within certain parameters, so they will search GuideStar to find them. If you fit their profile for location, mission, and programming, you may get an unexpected grant.

MacKenzie Scott, the former wife of Amazon founder Jeff Bezos, has given away about $13 billion to more than 1,200 nonprofits.[61] It is a mystery as to how she chooses them, but she has acknowledged that her team helps her to identify potential grant recipients. If your organization has what they are looking for, the more places you can be found by them or others, the better.

---

[61] ("The Mystery Of MacKenzie Scott: How and Why She Picks Certain Nonprofits Is A Puzzle, Even To Them" by Rachel Sandler [November 9, 2022]) Forbes.com https://www.forbes.com/sites/rachelsandler/2022/11/09/the-mystery-of-mackenzie-scott-how-and-why-she-picks-certain-nonprofits-is-a-puzzle-even-to-them/?sh=62e041a85659

## Website

Having a good website is imperative for credibility today. In addition to searching for your organization on GuideStar, people will go to your website to learn more about you. If you do not have a website, or if it is outdated and looks sad, it will reflect poorly on your organization. In many instances, your website is the first interaction people will have with your nonprofit, so you want to make a good first impression.

It is important to use a reputable, experienced website developer who can build a secure, compliant, and engaging website that includes best practices such as HTTP Strict Transport Security, site-wide SSL, and a compliant cookie banner.[62] Some states (and other countries) require you to get informed consent before the visitor enters your site if you intend to capture some of their personal data when they visit.

You may be able to find a volunteer with website expertise to create your website, you may barter in some way to arrange for someone to create it (sponsorship at your event, on the website, or other recognition), or you may want to pay to hire an expert. An expert can give you a polished look while also ensuring that you have a registered, secure website.

Use a website platform and a good web host that is secure. If you want people to find your website through Google, you need to use modern digital marketing best practices like **Search Engine Optimization (SEO).**[63] SEO is the process of growing a website's organic search traffic. The aim is to rank higher than similar search results so people will be directed to your website before your competition's website. This can be done by researching which keywords people search for, crafting website content that aligns with those keywords, and making sure your content is as clear as possible. This all starts with a domain name that fits with your organization, is findable, and is easy to recognize and trust.

Your website can be a very simple single page, or it can have multiple tabs, each with different information. If you have more than one page, your landing page should be short and to the point but friendly and welcoming. You do not want to overwhelm visitors with everything all at once. Give them a quick overview, your mission and core values, ads for upcoming events, and, of course, links for them to sign up for your newsletter or to volunteer. You may want to include some photos of recent events that include some well-known members of your community.

---

[62] ("Website Security Checklist: Protect Your Website in 2023" [January 8, 2023]) UpGuard https://www.upguard.com/blog/the-website-security-checklist

[63] ("SEO Basics: Beginner's Guide to SEO Success" by Joshua Hardwick [September 6, 2022]) ahrefs blog https://ahrefs.com/blog/seo-basics/

Be sure to have your contact information, including mailing address, phone, and email address easily findable on each page of the website. You should also make it clear at the bottom of every tab that your organization is a 501(c)(3) nonprofit, and donations are "tax deductible to the extent of the law." You may want list your EIN number somewhere since many employers require an EIN to provide matching funds for employee contributions.

All other pages should be easily accessible through the tabs at the top or side of the page, clearly-marked links elsewhere on the page, or both. Include an "About" page that gives a short history of how the organization was formed; your organizational structure; a list of board members, advisory council members, and staff members with their photos and short bios; and any other overview information about your charity. Other tabs may include your organizational policies, annual reports, contact information for specific people or sections of the nonprofit, job postings, and information about your programs.

You may want to add a tab with details for an upcoming event with links to register, sponsor the event, or volunteer to help. Be sure to include all of the event details like date, time, and location. Hide this tab a month or so after the event so your website does not look dated if someone visits it months later. On this tab and most of the others, be sure to include a "Donate" button to make it easy if people are inspired to donate after learning more about the great mission you are serving.

## Database

In your early days, your email/mailing list will likely be a spreadsheet or multiple spreadsheets where you keep the names and contact information of interested parties. This may include your board members, volunteers, and donors or potential donors.

As you grow, your spreadsheets should morph into an online database for a number of reasons. Once you have obtained the coveted contact information, you do not want to misplace it. You will also want to have more than one person able to access the most up-to-date information, and you do not want to have some members of your organization using outdated versions of the spreadsheet. You may want to start by using **Google Workspace**. It includes Gmail email, Calendar, Meet, Chat, Drive, Docs, Sheets, Slides, Forms, Sites, and more. When you create documents in Google Docs or save existing documents there, multiple people can access and work on them at the same time, with changes saved automatically. There are many tutorials online to help you learn how best to use it for your organization.

You may later move from free software to paying for a database. A database can allow read-only access for some people and full access for others, so only those who are entrusted with updating or changing the entries have that ability. Being able to link your database to your giving platform will add new members (and their contact information) to the database each time someone donates or registers for an event.

A Customer Relationship Management (CRM) software package is a central database that can manage contacts, donors, and other supporters, consolidating all of the information in a central location. It is a type of donor management software that helps you maximize your relationships and outreach, track constituents, manage donations, and streamline communications.

Each nonprofit organization is unique and will have unique needs for the types of data they need to store and organize, so be sure to compare and contrast the different types of options available. Many vendors offer different levels of support and storage capacity at different price points. Choose the one that is right for you now, but that can also grow with you. Try to find a CRM that has integrations built in with the other programs you may already be using for payment processing, email marketing, and fundraising, so the transition is a bit more seamless.

Once a database is chosen, it will take time, effort, and a bit of growing pains to input all of your data. Thought should go into all of the fields you will require and the layouts of the different pages so your staff and volunteers can easily access the information and run the reports they will need. The software vendor may offer an option where they will input your data, but your spreadsheets will need to be organized and sorted in a way that it will be correctly accepted into the database. Spending time up front to organize the data that will be uploaded will save your team hours of work later.

Of course, a database, like any other computerized tool, is only as good as the information fed into it. Your organization will need at least one person dedicated to managing the database. Reports will occasionally highlight errors in the way data has been input, so care is needed to immediately correct the bad data. Brief those who have input access on the proper procedures to avoid future problems.

If you do an online search for "Best Nonprofit Database Software," you will find a number of organizations that will help you compare to find one that best fits your needs. You may need to give them your name, organization name, and contact information to access the comparison tools.

## Email Outreach

Whether you have a spreadsheet or a database, you will want to start gathering names and contact information (mailing address, email address, and phone number) right away. Constant Contact, Mailchimp, and similar programs are a great way to create and send emails to those on your lists. They allow you to create the email's body content (with any links to online sites embedded), attach the list of email addresses you would like to send it to, and schedule a time and date for it to be sent. There are plenty of other email marketing tools out there for nonprofits, so shop around for your best fit.[64]

If you send a direct email to a group, be sure to always use the "BCC" (blind carbon copy) line for your list of email addresses. You need to be careful not to publicly share private email addresses with the other addressees. Potential donors may unsubscribe or express their displeasure in other ways if they feel you have violated their privacy.

Coordinate your efforts so you are not overwhelming your email recipients. All team/committee members need to coordinate their outreach ahead of time to be sure your organization looks like one cohesive unit. You do not want each contact receiving disparate emails from multiple segments of the same nonprofit, seemingly at the same time.

Your Social Media & Marketing team should plan a schedule of outreach, so your donors do not feel like you constantly have your hand out. There should be one or two giving campaigns each year with an announcement email and two or three reminders before the giving deadline. The president may want to keep everyone informed about the work you are doing by sending an **update email** every few months, and you should also put together a **newsletter** with highlights of your programs and a community report that goes out quarterly or at least twice a year. An **annual report** showing the income, donors, and accomplishments will go out annually, ideally within the first quarter after your fiscal year end (or as soon as you have the financial information from an annual audit). **Event invitations** should be first emailed at least two months prior to the event, with reminders sent every few weeks until the event.

You may decide to (snail) mail some of the above items, but there may be many people in your database who you only have an email address for, with no street

---

[64] ("Email Marketing for Nonprofits: 10 Top Tools for Your Organization [August 5, 2022]) The Ascent (a Motley Fool service) https://www.fool.com/the-ascent/small-business/email-marketing/articles/email-marketing-for-nonprofits/

address, so you will want to send both. Be mindful that some people will be receiving a physical invitation or solicitation letter and an email. Word the email carefully to let those people know you are emailing to make it easy to sign up or donate by including the links in the email.

It is required by law that you include an **opt-out link** in any unsolicited commercial emails (newsletters, letter from the president, ads for your event, etc.) that you send, so the receiver may opt out of receiving any in the future.[65] Your email outreach program should notify you of these opt-outs as they come in, so you can be sure to remove them from your outreach lists.

## Giving Platform

Your organization's giving platform will track donors and process donation and registration payments. This works best when you also integrate the platform with your database, social media platforms, and website. Fund development tools like **Network for Good** allow you to track donor levels, integrate with your website, process payments, and give you ad campaigns to use on your social media channels. The right database software program will help you increase donor retention, and some have a connection with **Constant Contact** or other communications tools, so it is very easy to connect the email addresses in your database to the emails you create and send.

## Social Media

Social media should be a part of your overall communications plan. It is essential for community engagement and brand awareness. It can help generate donations and volunteers and broaden your reach. Your communications standards should be made clear to anyone who has the authority to post.

The different platforms will help you disseminate information quickly to a global audience and will enable you to get continuous feedback. If you are able to adapt as the technological preferences of the population you are trying to reach change, it will help your organization stay relevant.

In addition to your website, people will look at your social media content if they want to learn more about your organization. Check out the social media pages for other nonprofits to get ideas about what to do and what not to do. You will know it when you see it.

---

[65] (CAN-SPAM Act: A Compliance Guide for Business [edited January 2022]) Federal Trade Commission https://www.ftc.gov/business-guidance/resources/can-spam-act-compliance-guide-business

You may use volunteers for this effort when you are starting out, but you will most likely need hired help as your organization and the need to better manage your outreach grows. It takes a continuous concerted effort to create new content, regularly post on multiple channels, and monitor and respond to comments and questions. Identify your media team early. Do not assume that only your youngest board members or interns will be natural social media strategists. Many organizations offer tips and training for social media, so seek them out to learn more about timing and content of posts, different platforms, strategies, etc.

The social media team should have a strategic communications calendar that includes dates for all outreach, including different social media platforms, email, and board communications. The calendar should also include when to update the website, add event pages, and create links for online registration or raffle ticket purchases.

Social media channels should be used to drive awareness of and engagement with your organization, but it can also be a great tool to grow your email list. You can invite followers to subscribe to your newsletter or other information outreach options, and as they subscribe, they will be required to enter their name and email address. You can also use social media to invite people to visit your website to learn more. They may click the links to sign up for a newsletter, register for an event, or give you their contact information for some other reason.

"Likes" on a social media platform are great, but your ultimate goal is to drive readers to action like volunteering, donating, or signing up for an event. Create a written social media policy that defines why your organization is using the platforms, on which platforms you will post, and who your target audience should be for each platform.

The type and timing of your social media posts will depend on the platform and the demographic of its users. You may need to do A/B testing on each channel, posting on different days and different times of day to compare the interaction you receive. Post on the same day of the week/time for a few weeks, then change and compare after a few weeks. You may also find research data for your industry that shows you the best time to post on a given platform. In general, the peak usage/viewing times are when people get up in the morning, when they go to lunch, on their commute home from work, and before bed at night.

Your mission and purpose should drive how you use social media. Use the platforms where your likely donors can be reached, and build content specifically for the different audiences that use each platform. Social Media posting takes work, and you should be creating different content for each of the channels. Integrated Marketing, which is placing the same content on many different platforms, has been proven not to work on social media, so you need to be more strategic with content on different platforms. This means that your media team may be running multiple campaigns at once. There are many different platforms to choose from.

**LinkedIn** is a professional networking tool. Most people are not logging in every day, so you may want to post once a week. Many elected officials have LinkedIn accounts, so you may be able to engage them in your topic here. You may only join groups or participate in conversations as an individual, not as an organization, so have your staff members create their own pages. It is very important to have a clear communications policy so they understand what they may post when representing the organization.

LinkedIn also has a "Learning" tab that is an online educational platform that has more than 5,000 courses on most business-related fields and interests. You may find helpful courses for your nonprofit.

**Facebook** users tend to check their accounts every day. Users on Facebook will click through to other pages like your website or other "offsite" locations, so consider adding links in your posts. Your organization can qualify to have a nonprofit account that can have multiple administrators, but you will need to submit all of your foundational documents to prove that you are a legitimate 501(c)(3) nonprofit.

**Instagram** is mostly a "scrolling" site where users will only stop on beautiful photos that capture their attention. This is not the place for long, wordy posts or graphics. You can add multiple choice or fill-in-the-blank response options for people to engage with your post and give you a bit of feedback on how they are feeling at that moment or how they feel about a particular topic. Instagram Stories will disappear after 24 hours while Posts will last forever. Use Stories to post items that are happening today or tomorrow.

Additional social media/online communications options are **YouTube, TikTok, X, Snapchat,** and others that are or will be on the horizon. You do not have to be on every channel. In fact, you are much better off if you pick just two or three and focus your efforts there. When a new platform emerges as the "in place," your organization does not need to be the first there (but you may want to claim your name for future use on that channel). You may expend a lot of effort to get a post out that only 10 people see. Use your time wisely.

Many nonprofits rely on their board members to share posts to their own feeds to try to increase visibility. This should also be used sparingly because not all board members are tech savvy or have an online presence, and they may experience social media burnout if you are pushing them to share things every week or every month. For the occasions that you do want your board to amplify your social media messages, make it very easy for them to share the post, or maybe send them an email from the president with a hyperlink to the newsletter or shareable item. You could email them a picture, PDF, or invitation with all of the details they can just forward or easily copy and paste.

One social media expert told me how she created a clickable PDF with specific actions board members could take each day for a number of days before an event. This went over so well that the national chapter of the nonprofit adopted it for the following year. You could create a "Social Media Tool Kit" for board members that spells out how they can be helpful in sharing the information.

Create content that moves your audience to act and has clear calls to action. Be relatable and authentic with interesting posts.

**Canva.com** may be used to create social media content and to schedule your posts for a later time, and it is free to nonprofit organizations. (You may also use Canva to create workflow charts, presentations, letterhead, resumes, and other work-related creative content.) Consider working with influencers or creators to leverage their audiences to broaden your reach.

If you add hashtags (#) or tag people (@) in your posts, you may reach more people. A hashtag is searchable, so someone looking for a particular topic may find your post, but it could be at a much later date. If you tag people, their friends or links may also see your post, and those people may share it on their pages, so you may reach additional people that way.

Posts should try to engage a two-way conversation and not just be a soliloquy. Stay away from controversial issues, so you do not lose some of your followers. Try posting things about your work and mission that tug on people's heartstrings. Provide information, express gratitude, list volunteer opportunities (and make it easy to sign up), and post photos of fun group projects rather than constantly asking people to donate.

Your "organic reach" is how many people will see your online content without boosting it by paying for ads. On Facebook, it is estimated that about 2-8% of your followers will actually see what you post. This is because of the Facebook algorithm[66] that determines which posts people will see when they check their feed, and also because different people will check at different times, so your post may get buried.

You can pay for ads on Facebook, Instagram, LinkedIn, and other platforms. Ads can target a specific audience by gender, age, location, or topic, but the specifics are different on each platform. The most effective way to reach your target audience will be to pay for ads, not by organic reach or "sharing" of your posts. This may also take some trial and error to determine the best return for your ad dollars.

Define your objectives and goals up front for what you want to accomplish this fiscal year on social media. Choose your data collection tools to quantify, measure, and interpret results. Use Key Performance Indicators (KPIs) to quantify and measure the performance over time for a particular objective. Think about how many people you want to send to your website from your social media platforms, or how many volunteers you want to sign up through your social media posts. These KPIs should be reported to the board on a regular basis, and adjustments can be made if your goals are not being met.

What worked when you started may change, so you need to constantly re-evaluate and adjust your social media strategy. Our world and our technology are constantly changing, so your social media strategy will need to be adjusted at times to continue to be effective.

## Conferencing Platforms & Firewalls

Some companies you may want to conference with have computer firewalls that prevent their employees from accessing certain apps or platforms. **Google Meet,** a video-communication service, and **Zoom,** another cloud-based video conferencing service where you meet using audio, video, or both (the conferencing software that most people got familiar with during the pandemic) may both be blocked by some firewalls, so you may need to use **Microsoft Teams** or another platform instead.

**Microsoft Teams** is a business communication platform that offers workspace chat and videoconferencing, file storage, and application integration. Teams integrates with Microsoft Office 365 tools. It became widely used during the COVID-19 pandemic because it allows teams to coordinate their efforts, work together and apart on different projects, upload files, edit simultaneously, and

---

[66] ("2023 Facebook Algorithm: How to Get Your Content Seen" by Christina Newberry [February 22, 2023]) Houtsuite https://blog.hootsuite.com/facebook-algorithm/

has chat features. It allows setup of different "team channels" for each project. Those in the team channel can ping each other in the chat, and the chats are saved, so they may be referenced later. There is a calendar feature for scheduling. When using the video team meeting feature, it is easy to share content because it is already integrated.

## Other Handy Helpers

We have come a long way in the area of apps and software that make our jobs easier, help us communicate better (within the organization and outside of it), and manage our schedules. The options change every day, so I am going to list only a few here to give you an idea of some of the help that is out there.

The cloud-based options allow for peace of mind in storing valuable documents and allowing access to multiple users. Some offer additional features such as sharing or scheduling, making collaboration easier. Many offer free versions and upgrades with a paid subscription.

As with any tools used by your organization, there should always be a person or team of people responsible for its use. A plan should be in place as to how it is organized, who has access and what level of access, and how it shall be used.

As your needs and end users vary, you should research these options to find those that work best for your organization. Please note that the listings below are not endorsements for any specific products. They are listed in alphabetical order.

**Benevity** is a Canadian B Corp that has resources for nonprofits. They help "you access support from 750+ of the world's most iconic brands and their 20 million people, through giving, volunteering and grantmaking."

**Calendly** allows teams and individuals to schedule, prepare, and follow up on external meetings. Users share open time slots in their calendars to book meetings. You may customize how and when you are booked and can connect up to six calendars per user. You may also create meeting polls to find times most people are available.

**Doodle** is an online poll that helps with scheduling meetings and other events. The organizer fills in the details of the event and selects a number of dates and times that could work. The poll is then emailed to all potential attendees to fill in their availability. It becomes quickly evident, with the tallies for each time, when the majority of people are able to attend.

**Dropbox** is a cloud file hosting service that offers cloud storage, file synchronization, and additional services. Files may be easily sorted and arranged as if on an individual's desktop.

**Evite** is a social-planning website for creating, sending, and managing online event invitations. It also offers digital greeting cards and announcements. This may be a good option for inviting a list of people to smaller (less than 75 people) events.

**Google Drive** is a file storage and synchronization service. It allows users to store files, synchronize files across different devices, and share files. Multiple users may edit a file in real time.

**Hootsuite** is a social media management platform. It supports social network integrations for Twitter, Facebook, Instagram, LinkedIn, Pinterest, and YouTube. The basic service is free, and they have workshops and trainings to learn more about social media postings.

**Microsoft Excel** is a spreadsheet software that features calculation capabilities, graphing tools, sorting options, and pivot tables. An Excel spreadsheet can serve as your early database that holds names and contact information of donors and other stakeholders, your budget spreadsheet, and the keeper and organizer of other important data such as program outcomes and impact.

As mentioned in Chapter 6 and earlier in this chapter, there are many good reasons to move from a spreadsheet to a donor customer relationship management (CRM) database as soon as possible. Of course, Excel will still be valuable for creating financial statements and doing other organizational analysis.

**Microsoft OneNote** is a note-taking program for information gathering and for multi-user collaboration. It can gather all notes, drawings, screen clippings or screen captures, and audio commentaries. Data is saved automatically as the user makes edits to a file, but you may save versions along the way to keep a track record.

Pages are organized within broader notebooks, with the idea of it being like a virtual ring binder, and you can create different notebooks for each project, client, or board meeting. You may date stamp your pages to create a time sheet and proof of work for specific projects.

**QuickBooks** is online accounting software. It allows you to create invoices, track cash flow, accept payments, prepare financial statements, and can connect to your bank accounts.

**SharePoint** is a web-based collaborative platform that integrates with Microsoft Office. It is mostly used as a document management and storage system, but there are additional uses for it.

**Skype** is a telecommunications application that is a division of Microsoft. It is best known for videoconferencing and voice calls, but also has instant messaging, file transfer, and other features.

**Slack** is a messaging communications program designed for the workplace. It offers chat rooms organized by topic, private groups, one-on-one conversations, and direct messaging.

**WhatsApp** is an internationally available instant messaging and voice-over-IP (VoIP) service. Users may send text and voice messages, make voice and video calls, and share images or documents. It requires a mobile number to use. Users may make data-free calls and texts worldwide when connected to wi-fi.

Some of the software and apps provide file storage, while others only offer ways to communicate. Research the above and other options to see which will give your organization the right coverage.

# CHAPTER 12

# MERGING OR DISSOLVING

*"Now this is not the end. It is not even the beginning of the end.
But it is, perhaps, the end of the beginning."*

Winston Churchill
(British statesman, orator, and author)

## Merging

After a number of years of successfully running your organization, the board may find there is a similar organization in the area, and, for economies of scale or to save the least successful of the two nonprofits if one is starting to fail, the organizations should merge. There are positive and negative methods to accomplish this, but with a lot of thought and planning, the effort can be successful.

It may take a lot of headaches and heartaches working to develop the procedures and strategies for the termination of one organization and reorganization of the other. Both parties need to go into the process with complete transparency and an understanding of what the new culture and mission should look like. Once the details are worked out at all levels, the boards can determine which, if any, staff members and board members will be retained from the merged nonprofits. There may be some growing pains at first, but it can be the beginning of a new and improved mission delivery system.

## Dissolving

Dissolving a nonprofit may happen for a number of reasons, some positive and some not. If you have accomplished the mission you set out to accomplish, congratulations! This is the best reason of all to shut down your nonprofit.

Maybe you have grown, changed, or morphed, and you are merging with another like-minded organization. This is also a positive step, and you can hopefully find economies of scale in your combined organization.

It could be that the organization is no longer needed. It may have outlived its usefulness or become obsolete. If the organization is no longer actively fulfilling its mission, if the founder and the board are no longer actively engaged or focused on the mission, and the organization is not performing a function, it is time to shut it down.

There are also times when the nonprofit regulations are too restrictive for what the organization has become. It could realize more growth and could better contribute to the state's economy if it were to become a for-profit organization. In this case, the Attorneys General in each state in which you are operating will need to sign off on the conversion, so they will dictate the steps you will need to take.

## Dissolution Steps

Dissolution is not as easy as you may think. First, you need to be sure the organization is in "good standing," that all bills, taxes, and fees are paid in full and that all outstanding checks have cleared your bank account. This process may take weeks or months.

Once all the financial obligations are taken care of, you will need to go to the corporate website for the state in which you are incorporated and research what is required for corporate dissolution. A fee may be required in order to file. Keep copies of all paperwork for your records.

After the corporation dissolution paperwork is filed, go to IRS.gov and file your final 990. Fill out the forms, and **click the box that affirms that you are no longer in business**. Submit the form and print the confirmation for your records.

You may want to announce on your social media platforms and/or your website what is happening with your organization. Cancel any contracts that are set to renew.

You most likely pay for your website hosting platform and domain name(s) annually, so you will need to cancel the renewals and shut down the website when it is appropriate. Be sure to close down all social media channels.

Leave enough cash in the bank account to cover any dissolution fees and bank fees. Once all checks have cleared, you may write checks to qualifying nonprofits to clear out the account. Your bylaws should state the type of organizations that qualify to receive your remaining assets in accordance with the provisions of Section 501(c)(3) of the Internal Revenue Code. When these final checks have cleared, close the bank account. Dissolving may be sad or bittersweet, but know that closing or merging is not failure. Move on to help others in a new way.

# EPILOGUE/CONCLUSION

Starting and successfully running a charitable organization is a noble calling. It takes a lot of drive, commitment, and sweat equity. Our country would be lost without nonprofits – they are doing so much good!

I honor those of you out there doing the hard work to fulfill all of these worthy missions. I appreciate that you care so deeply.

Thank you for reading *So, You Want to Start a Nonprofit, Now What?* I would love to get your feedback. Please leave a book review on Amazon or wherever you purchased the book.

Also, feel free to keep in touch via my website: www.501Guide.com.

# ACKNOWLEDGMENTS

I would like to thank my village for helping me write this book and get it out into the world. There are scores of people who each contributed in some way, and it would not be as comprehensive without every one of them.

I want to give special thanks to Cheryl Moralez for designing the book cover, the pyramid graphics in Chapters 5 and 8, and the sample organizational chart in Appendix V. I also want to thank my beta readers Stephanie, Barb, Karla, Ann, Tom, Bert, and Kay.

I interviewed more than 60 people in Delaware and across the country who broadened my nonprofit knowledge. Others gave suggestions that helped greatly, and some even took the time to read the book and give early feedback. I tried very hard not to omit anyone, but if I did, please know that I am grateful for your help, too.

| Bonnie Adler | Data Privacy Senior Manager with Zaviant Consulting; former Data Privacy Consultant for Deloitte and TrustArc; former Chief Privacy Officer at The Chemours Company; Fund for Women at the Delaware Community Foundation Grants Committee member; Secretary of the Forum of Executive Women Delaware board | Pennsylvania |
|---|---|---|
| Maria Aristigueta | Dean & Charles P. Messick Chair in Public Administration of the Biden School of Public Policy and Administration at University of Delaware | Delaware |
| Carol Arnott Robbins | Head of NEWS 4 Women (Network to Encourage Women's Support) and Wine4Women events; Business Manager at White Robbins Property Management; Realtor at Berkshire Hathaway HomeServices Fox & Roach, Realtors | Delaware |
| Signe Bell | Director of Nonprofit Programs at University of Delaware, Biden School of Public Policy & Administration | Delaware |
| Sheila Bravo | Treasurer of National Council of Nonprofits board, President & CEO of the Delaware Alliance for Nonprofit Advancement (DANA); former Executive Director of Rehoboth Art League | Delaware |
| Callan Brown | Program Director at Nonprofit Center of Northeast Florida and the lead on their quarterly "How to Start a Nonprofit" program | Florida |
| Paul Calistro | Executive Director of West End Neighborhood House (DE); former Mayor of Newport, DE | Delaware |

| | | |
|---|---|---|
| Cheryl Christiansen | Retired Executive Director of Family Promise of Northern New Castle County (DE); former President of the Delaware Association of Volunteer Administrators board | Delaware |
| Rick Cohen | Chief Communications Officer/Chief Operating Officer of National Council of Nonprofits | Washington, DC |
| Stuart Comstock-Gay | President & CEO of Delaware Community Foundation | Delaware |
| Ed Cortas | Vice President of Strategic Initiatives and Consulting with the Center for Nonprofit Excellence in Louisville, KY | Kentucky |
| Stephanie Cory | Consultant/Facilitator/Trainer with Stephanie Cory Consulting – nonprofit consulting; BoardSource Certified Governance Consultant; Standards for Excellence licensed consultant; Association of Fundraising Professionals (AFP) Member | Delaware |
| Chris Crothers | Director of Impact Investing at Jessie Ball du Pont Fund; former Communications Director at Foundation for the Mid-South | Florida |
| Denée Crumrine | Corporate Communications, Community Affairs and Giving for Highmark Health; former Communications Manager for the Delaware State Chamber of Commerce; former Young Professionals Board Member at Junior Achievement of Delaware | Delaware |
| Patty Dailey Lewis | CEO of The Beau Biden Foundation for the Protection of Children; Adjunct Professor at Delaware Law School; former Deputy Attorney General for the Delaware Department of Justice | Delaware |

| | | |
|---|---|---|
| Fred Dawson | *Pearls* series of books author; Executive Vice President of Bassett, Dawson & Foy, Inc. financial planners | Delaware |
| Susan Detwiler | President of The Detwiler Group, Consultant for the Delaware Alliance for Nonprofit Advancement (DANA), Faculty Member at Creating the Future, Licensed Standards for Excellence Consultant, former Sr. Consultant for Bloom Metz Consulting, former Chair of Fund for Women at the Delaware Community Foundation Governance & Grants Committees | Delaware |
| Brian DiSabatino | Chair of Grand Opera House's "$10 Million Imagine Your Grand" Campaign (DE); former Chair of St. Francis Hospital Foundation (DE) board; Executive Committee Member of St. Francis Hospital Board; Vice Chair of Grand Opera House board; Director for Delaware State Chamber of Commerce; Past Chair of Chester County (PA) Chamber of Commerce; board member of Delaware Contractors Assoc., and Trustee of the American College in Dublin, Ireland | Delaware |
| Natalie DiSabatino | Community Affairs Specialist at Fortune 500 Company; former Campaign Manager at The Leukemia & Lymphoma Society; former Guest Services Assistant/Development Assistant at the Ronald McDonald House of Delaware | Delaware |

| | | |
|---|---|---|
| Carole Downs | Senior Loan Officer at NVR Mortgage; former Home Mortgage Consultant at Wells Fargo Mortgage; former Child Inc. (DE) board member & event planner; St. Lucia (Caribbean) preschool library co-founder; Haiti Family Initiative founding member | Florida |
| Thère du Pont | President of Longwood Foundation; serves on boards of DuPont Company, WSFS Bank, and Burris Logistics; Board Chair of both Pete du Pont Freedom Foundation and Community Education Building; former Senior Vice President of Operations & CFO of drugstore.com; former President and CFO of Wawa, Inc. | Delaware |
| Temeka Easter Rice | Head of Social Media at Vanguard; Owned The Joy Group doing branding, social media & marketing; former Senior Director of Social Media at Sallie Mae | Delaware |
| Sharmina Ellis | Career Elevation Liaison at Tech Impact (F/T), Executive Director at EDGE For Tomorrow (P/T), Adjunct Instructor at Wilmington University, Higher Education and Workforce Consultant | Delaware |
| Drew Fennell | Retired Senior Vice President, Chief Officer of Strategic Communication and Development at ChristianaCare Health System; former Chief of Staff for Delaware Governor Jack Markell; Attorney; Advocate | Delaware |

| Allison Fine | Author of *The Smart Nonprofit: Staying Human-Centered in an Automated World, Matterness: What Fearless Leaders Know About the Power and Promise of Social Media, and Momentum: Igniting Social Change in the Connected Age*; Founder of Innovation Network in Washington, DC (innonet.org) | New York |
|---|---|---|
| Brother Ronald Giannone | Founder & Executive Director of The Ministry of Caring Inc. | Delaware |
| Molly Giordano | Executive Director of the Delaware Art Museum; Vice Chair & former Governance Chair of Fund for Women at the Delaware Community Foundation | Delaware |
| Guillermina Gonzalez | Assistant Professor of the College of Business & Assistant Chair of Undergraduate Programs at Wilmington University (DE); former Executive Director of Delaware Arts Alliance; former Executive Director of Voices Without Borders | Delaware |
| Carrie Gray | Founder & Principal at Gray Breakthroughs, LLC – coaching & consulting; Co-owner of Griswold Home Care (New Castle County DE) former Director of the College of Business & Chair of the Doctor of Business Administration Program at Wilmington University; President of Delaware Theatre Company board | Delaware |
| Sarah Green | Executive Director of Pacem in Terris Delaware; former Director of Community Engagement at Literacy Delaware; former Program Coordinator for Refugee Integration Support Effort at Jewish Family Services of Delaware; Founder and original Executive Director of Urban Bike Project | Delaware |

| | | |
|---|---|---|
| Chris Grundner | President & CEO of Welfare Foundation, Inc.; former President & CEO of Delaware Alliance for Nonprofit Advancement; Founder and former Executive Director of The Kelly Heinz-Grundner Brain Tumor Foundation; former Senior Vice President/Director of Business Development for JPMorgan Chase & Co. | Delaware |
| David Hannah | Academic Program Coordinator at University of Delaware; Secretary of the African Heritage Caucus at University of Delaware | Delaware |
| Harvard Business School "Preparing to Be a Corporate Director" small group | Individuals from Boston (Sheila), Brazil (Lauro), Louisville (Tess), New York (Chris), and Saudi Arabia (Mohammed), who have supported me from the start | Massachusetts, Kentucky, New York, Brazil, & Saudi Arabia |
| Logan Herring | CEO of WRK Group (The Warehouse, REACH Riverside, & Kingswood Community Center); former Statewide STEAM (STEM + Arts) Program Coordinator at Boys & Girls Club of Delaware; board member of Community Education Building and Goodwill of Delaware and Delaware County | Delaware |
| Lois Hoffman | Owner of The Happy Self Publisher | Delaware |
| Lisa-Marie Jackson | Co-Founder & CEO of Sociable Consulting digital marketing agency; former Social Media Leadership at Trellist Marketing and Technology; former Social Business Strategist at Sallie Mae; President-Elect & Digital Media Chair on Fresh Start Scholarship Foundation board | Delaware |

| Hon. Kent Jordan | Judge of 3rd Circuit Court of Appeals in Philadelphia, Adjunct Professor of Law at Vanderbilt University and University of Pennsylvania, ecclesiastical leader of Church of Jesus Christ of Latter-Day Saints in Delaware, The Ministry of Caring Inc. board member | Pennsylvania |
|---|---|---|
| Kay Keenan | Project Faculty for Executive MBA students at The Wharton School, University of Pennsylvania; President of Growth Consulting helping for-profit and nonprofit businesses; Co-Author of *Conversation on Networking*; former Vice President of Marketing and Communications at Big Brothers Big Sisters of America; Chair of the Fund for Women at the Delaware Community Foundation board and Secretary of Goodwill of Delaware and Delaware County board | Delaware |
| Kristi Krings | CEO of Rachel's Challenge; former Sr. Strategic Partner Manager for Omnichannel Marketplaces; former Global Head of Partnerships (The Launchpad Initiative) for UNiDAYS; International UNiDAYS Influencer of the Year 2017 | Colorado |
| Pamela Leland | Chief Learning Officer at Delaware Alliance for Nonprofit Advancement; Self-employed Consultant/Adviser/Coach for mission-driven organizations | Delaware |
| Anya Lindsey-Jenkins | Executive Director of Big Brothers Big Sisters of Delaware; former Director at West End Neighborhood House; Get a GRIP Teen Mentoring Workshop board member | Delaware |

| Chris Locke | General Counsel/Senior Vice President of Lang Development Group; Founder and President of SL24: Unlocke the Light Foundation/Sean's House | Delaware |
|---|---|---|
| Karla Lodholz | Director of Member Relations & Resource Development at Wisconsin Philanthropy Network; former Director of Donor Services at Community Foundation of North Central Wisconsin; former Regional VP of American Heart Association | Wisconsin |
| Ann Marinangeli | Vice President/IT Project Manager at Chase; former VP at MBNA America; Fund for Women at the Delaware Community Foundation Founder; Adopt-a-Family volunteer | Pennsylvania |
| Pamela Martin Turner | President & CEO of Vanguard Community Development Corporation (Detroit); former Senior Tax Attorney at the IRS; former Adjunct Lecturer at the University of Michigan's Graduate School of Social Work | Michigan |
| Joe McDonough | Founder & President of The Andrew McDonough B+ ("Be Positive") Foundation; former Senior Vice President at JPMorgan Chase | Delaware |
| Mary McDonough | Commissioner of Delaware Court of Common Pleas; The Ministry of Caring Inc. (DE) board member; Policy Director of Delaware Anti-Trafficking Action Council (DATAC) | Delaware |
| Jerry McGeorge | Executive Vice President of People at Organic Valley; former Chair, Vice Chair, and Treasurer of the National Cooperative Business Association board | Wisconsin |

| Adele McIntosh | CPA & Partner of Daniels + Tansey, LLP's tax group; Treasurer of Delaware Nature Society board; former Treasurer and President of Rotary Club of Brandywine (DE) | Delaware |
|---|---|---|
| Vince McIntosh | Owner of Select Amenities Ltd.; experience in domestic and international sales and distribution, product launches, trade shows, and sales presentations | Delaware |
| Tess McNair | Executive Director at C.E. and S. Foundation (Louisville, KY); former Communications Manager & Special Advisor to the Chairman of the Board at Humana | Kentucky |
| Connie Montana | Environmental, Social and Governance (ESG) Program Manager, Senior Vice President at Bank of America; Delaware Council for Economic Education board member: active in financial literacy efforts | Delaware |
| Leslie Newman | Retired Executive Director at Children & Families First (DE); former President of Jewish Federation of Delaware | Delaware |
| Caron Ogg | National President of the ARCS Foundation (Achievement Rewards for College Scientists); started a public schools foundation in the Seattle area | Oregon |
| Larry Ogg | CEO and former Board Chair of Commerce Bank of Oregon and board member since the bank's inception in 2005; Retired as President of Bank of America's Oregon operations | Oregon |

| Barbara Hobday Owens | Retired attorney specializing in employment law, employee relations, health law, government contracts and procurement, administrative law, and mediation; certified as a Senior Professional in Human Resources; Sailing the world since 2016 | Texas |
|---|---|---|
| Louisa "Louie" Phillips | Grants Chair at Delaware Community Foundation; Retired Senior Director of Operations for the Cardiovascular Service Line at Bayhealth Medical Center; former Chair of Fund for Women at the Delaware Community Foundation board; Secretary of Bayhealth Foundation; Planned Parenthood of Delaware, Mary Ann's List, and Ready to Run Delaware board member | Delaware |
| Anthea Piscarik | Development Associate/Grant Writer for The Ministry of Caring; Author of *The Years in Between* (Book 2 of "The Miriam Chronicles" series) | Delaware |
| Nicole Poore | Delaware State Senator heading bond committee (Joint Committee on Capital Improvement), President of Jobs for Delaware Graduates nonprofit | Delaware |
| Cynthia Primo Martin | *Handbook for Nonprofit Leadership: Recruiting, Training and Engaging Trustees of Color* author; founder of the Trustees of Color (TOC) initiative; former Trustee/Board Member of University of Delaware, Delaware Community Foundation, and a number of other nonprofits | Delaware |

| Mark Reardon | Attorney & Co-Chair of Mass Tort Litigation Group at Eckert Seamans Cherin & Mellott, LLC; Commissioner for Board of Delaware River Pilot Commissioners; President of Ministry of Caring Inc. board | Delaware |
|---|---|---|
| Bill Ryan | Principal at Ryan Consulting Group (USA) and Adjunct Lecturer of Executive Education for Nonprofits at Harvard University's Kennedy School | Massachusetts |
| Laurisa Schutt | Executive Director of First State Educate; former Executive Director of Teach for America Delaware; on boards of St. Andrew's School (DE), Leadership Delaware, the Delaware Coalition Against Gun Violence, and UD's College of Education, and is Board Chair of 4th Dimension Leaders | Delaware |
| Kiersten Schwendeman | Executive Assistant to the Chief Executive Officer and Director at Quip Laboratories; Founder and former President of Aster Wellness Foundation | Delaware |
| Fred Sears | Retired President & CEO of Delaware Community Foundation; former President of Commerce Bank/Delaware; former Wilmington City Councilman; Chair of the Wilmington Economic and Financial Advisory Council; serves and has served on numerous nonprofit boards | Delaware |
| Sharece Sellem-Hannah | Advocate for the arts, mental health, and alternative education routes | Delaware |

| Nigel Smart | *Bouncing Back from Divorce with Purpose & Vitality* author; President of SMART Pharma Consulting, LLC | Pennsylvania |
|---|---|---|
| Thomas W. Smith | Corporate finance professional, experienced nonprofit board officer and member, and community volunteer | Pennsylvania |
| Betty Sweeny | President of Business Development Associates, Inc.; former Senior Vice President, Co-brand Marketing at The Bank of New York; President of the Fresh Start Scholarship Foundation board; former National MS Society, Delaware Chapter board member; Delaware Theatre Company board member | Delaware |
| Michelle Taylor | President & CEO of United Way of Delaware; Philanthropy Delaware board member; former CFO of Delaware Hospice | Delaware |
| Allison Taylor Levine | Vice President of Marketing & Communications at Delaware Community Foundation; President & Founder of Local Journalism Initiative (DE) | Delaware |
| Dave Tiberi | President of Emergency Response Protocol; Co-Founder of Donate Delaware; Inducted into Pennsylvania Boxing Hall of Fame & Delaware Sports Hall of Fame | Delaware |
| Greg Varallo | Partner at Bernstein Litowitz Berger & Grossmann LLP law firm; former Director/Corporate Litigator/ Firm President at Richards, Layton & Finger, P.A. law firm; former board president for The Ministry of Caring Inc. (DE) | Pennsylvania |

| | | |
|---|---|---|
| Charlie Vincent | Executive Director of Spur Impact - nonprofit that connects millennials/young professionals; Owner & Principal at Innovincent - helps nonprofits raise funds | Delaware |
| Jane C. W. Vincent | President of Delaware Public Media (went through rebranding, upgraded digital media and communications); appointed by President Obama as Regional Administrator for the US Department of Housing and Urban Development (HUD), overseeing all HUD activities within the Mid-Atlantic states; Adjunct faculty at University of Delaware | Delaware |
| Aida Waserstein | *My Name is Aida* author; retired Delaware Family Court Judge | Delaware |
| Robert Whetzel | Director at Richards, Layton & Finger, P.A.; board member at Stroud Water Research Center and Science, Technology and Research Institute of Delaware (STRIDE) | Delaware |
| Rita Wilkins | *Downsize Your Life, Upgrade Your Lifestyle: Secrets to More Time, Money, and Freedom* author; President/CEO/Interior Designer with Design Services, Ltd.; former President of Fresh Start Scholarship Foundation | Delaware |
| | | |

The following appendices contain samples of a certificate of incorporation, a budget, a business plan, and other helpful information. They are provided as a guide and are not meant to be universal to all organizations. Please research, plan, and adopt those standards and policies that will guide your specific nonprofit.

# APPENDIX I –
# RESOURCE ORGANIZATIONS

**General Nonprofit Assistance:**

- **Candid.org (Foundation Center & Guidestar joined forces)** gives information about nonprofits (you can research and verify nonprofits here), foundations, grants, and gaining visibility to attract donors.

- **Center for Nonprofit Excellence** serves as "a champion, learning partner, and advisor to nonprofits" – there are partnerships with many local nonprofit-related organizations. Do an online search to find one nearby.

- In Delaware the **Delaware Alliance for Nonprofit Advancement (DANA)** can:
  - ○ Provide statistics for nonprofits and different sectors
  - ○ Do consulting for emerging nonprofits
  - ○ Help create bylaws
  - ○ Help nonprofits think about what their plans are/should be
  - ○ Get the 1023 signed [application for recognition of exemption to apply for 501(c)(3)]
  - ○ Help with initial planning
  - ○ Give nonprofits an initial fundraising strategy
  - ○ Help existing nonprofits add staff, payroll, compensation or HR policies, or start to thrive if they are flailing https://delawarenonprofit.org/

- **Innovation Network** helps make evaluation accessible to nonprofits and foundations. https://innonet.org

- Get help with **Government Contracting** at https://www.sba.gov/federal-contracting/contracting-guide

- **Multi-State Registration:** Unified Registration is an effort to consolidate information and data requirements of all states that require registration of nonprofit organizations soliciting in their state (Colorado, Oklahoma, and Florida do not accept the URS, and 14 of them require supplementary forms) http://multistatefiling.org/

- **National Association of Black Nonprofits** has nonprofit resources for Black nonprofits and Black nonprofit professionals https://www.blacknonprofits.org/

- **National Association of State Charity Officials** is an association of state offices (attorneys general, secretaries of state, and other offices) charged with the regulation and oversight of charitable organizations in the U.S. It provides a forum for states to share information and collaborate on matters related to charities oversight. They have a list of organizations that provide resources for nonprofits. https://www.nasconet.org/resources/national-resources/

  The National Association of State Charity Officials (NASCOnet1) can also tell you how to **register as a nonprofit in each state to legally solicit funds in other states**. There is a state agency listed for each state. http://www.nasconet.org/resources/state-government/

- **National Center on Charitable Statistics** is a national clearinghouse of data on the nonprofit sector in the US. https://nccs.urban.org/

- **National Council of Nonprofits** works collaboratively to advance federal public policy for nonprofits but also helps support within the states. They offer a lot of resources - look for your local affiliate (or nonprofit state association). They also have information about which states require solicitation registration. https://www.councilofnonprofits.org/

  The National Council of Nonprofits also has a section on **games of chance, raffles, and charity auctions**. https://www.councilofnonprofits.org/tools-resources/games-of-chance-raffles-and-charity-auctions

- Get **free advice from business experts** through **SCORE** (Service Corps of Retired Executives) – a 501(c)(3) that is the largest network of volunteer expert business mentors (hundreds of locations around the country – more than 50 in Connecticut alone!) – can help with business plan, realistic goals and business needs and cost projections. www.score.org

- **Society for Nonprofits** is a membership organization that offers training and certifications. (https://www.snpo.org/)
- **Standards for Excellence Institute** – for nonprofits. Offers an A-Z resource on best practices for nonprofit organizational governance, management, policies, and procedures, and legal compliance at any stage of a nonprofit's lifecycle. You can become a member, and they can help you become accredited and/or find licensed consultants in your area. https://standardsforexcellence.org/
- **Sustainable Economies Law Center** has help and resources for setting up and running a worker self-directed nonprofit https://www.theselc.org/worker_selfdirected_nonprofits
- **United Nations Sustainable Development Goals** – there are 17 goals that came out of the United Nations Conference on Sustainable Development (https://sustainabledevelopment.un.org/content/documents/1579SDGs%20Proposal.pdf), and through the work aimed at reaching those goals, they have a lot of statistics and details about poverty, hunger, health, education, gender equality, etc. (https://sdgs.un.org/)
- **Wallace Foundation** is specifically for education and arts education, but they have "Financial Management for Nonprofits," "Framework for Measuring After School Programs," "Cross-Sector Collaboration," "Advancing Philanthropy," and other resources – free tutorials to do cash flow projection, budgeting, etc. www.wallacefoundation.org

**Technical Help:**

- **BoardSource** offers nonprofit board leadership research, leadership, and support. https://boardsource.org/
- **Keela** is a fundraising customer relationship management (CRM) platform that unifies fundraising and donor communications. They are a certified B-Corp, so they seek to help. www.keela.co (not a typo)
- **TechSoup** offers technology for nonprofits, charities, and libraries at a discount (QuickBooks, refurbished computers, Dell discounts, servers and networking devices, Microsoft Office, and more plus website development, digital marketing services, and courses for the U.S. and many other countries (must prove 501(c)(3) status or be a public library). https://www.techsoup.org/

**Subscriptions/Memberships:**

- **Nonprofit Quarterly** offers free and on-demand webinars. You can subscribe to their newsletters or become a member and have access to their full digital library. https://nonprofitquarterly.org/

- **Independent Sector** is membership organization that brings together a diverse community of changemakers at nonprofits, foundations, and corporate giving programs that helps build connections and offers programs to help their members better understand the current health of the nonprofit sector. https://independentsector.org/

- Nonprofit press: **The Chronicle of Philanthropy** https://www.philanthropy.com/subscribe/, **Inside Philanthropy** https://www.insidephilanthropy.com/

## Nonprofit Resources in Each State

This is by no means a comprehensive list. It was created by doing online searches, so I may have missed some. For some states, there are volunteer connection sites listed as well as nonprofit resource centers. Check https://www.councilofnonprofits.org/find-your-state-association for an up-to-date list of state nonprofit associations that are in the National Council of Nonprofits network.

- **Alabama**

  Alabama Association of Nonprofits:
  https://www.alabamanonprofits.org/
  Alabama Governor's Office of Volunteer Services:
  https://www.servealabama.gov/

- **Alaska**

  The Foraker Group:
  https://www.forakergroup.org/
  Chamber of Commerce: How to Start a Nonprofit in Alaska:
  https://www.chamberofcommerce.org/nonprofit/alaska
  Nonprofit Community Association Handbook:
  https://dot.alaska.gov/stwdplng/transit/pub/NonProfit_Community_Assoc_Handbook.pdf

- **Arizona**

  Alliance of Arizona Nonprofits:
  https://arizonanonprofits.org/
  Arizona Department of Economic Security: Volunteer Engagement Center:
  https://des.az.gov/how-do-i/volunteer-engagement-center

- **Arkansas**

  Arkansas Community Foundation:
  https://www.arcf.org/

- **California**

  CalNonprofits:
  https://calnonprofits.org/
  California Volunteers:
  https://www.facebook.com/CaliforniaVolunteers

- **Colorado**

  Colorado Nonprofit Association:
  https://coloradononprofits.org/
  Denver Volunteer Opportunities: https://www.denvergov.org/content/denvergov/
  en/denver-human-resources/volunteer-opportunities.html

- **Connecticut**

  The Alliance Voice of Community Nonprofits:

  https://ctnonprofitalliance.org/

- **Delaware**

  Delaware Alliance for Nonprofit Advancement:
  https://delawarenonprofit.org/
  State Office of Volunteerism:
  https://volunteer.delaware.gov/

- **Florida**

  Florida Association of Nonprofits:
  https://fano.org/
  Florida Nonprofit Alliance:
  https://flnonprofits.org/
  Volunteer Florida:
  https://www.volunteerflorida.org/

- **Georgia**

  Georgia Center for Nonprofits:
  https://gcn.org/
  Atlanta – Hands on Atlanta Americorps Team:
  https://www.handsonatlanta.org/

- **Hawaii**

  Hawaii Alliance of Nonprofit Organizations:
  https://hano-hawaii.org/

- **Idaho**

  Idaho Nonprofit Center:
  https://www.idahononprofits.org/
  Serve Idaho:
  https://serve.idaho.gov/

- **Illinois**

  Chicago Non-Profit Organizations:
  https://www.chicago.gov/city/en/ofinterest/bus/non_prof.html
  Illinois Department of Human Services: Volunteer Opportunities:
  https://www.dhs.state.il.us/page.aspx?item=30916

- **Indiana**

  Indiana Philanthropy Alliance:
  https://www.inphilanthropy.org/
  Serve Indiana:
  https://www.in.gov/serveindiana/

- **Iowa**

  The Larned A. Waterman Iowa Nonprofit Resource Center:
  https://inrc.law.uiowa.edu/
  Nonprofit Association of the Midlands, Iowa Nonprofit Alliance (serving Nebraska & Western Iowa):
  https://www.nonprofitam.org/members/?id=66025884
  Volunteer Iowa:
  https://www.volunteeriowa.org/

- **Kansas**

  Association of Kansas Nonprofits:
  https://kansasnonprofit.org/

- **Kentucky**

  Kentucky Nonprofit Network:
  https://www.kynonprofits.org/

- **Louisiana**

  Louisiana Alliance for Nonprofits:
  https://www.louisiananonprofits.org/

- **Maine**

  Maine Association of Nonprofits:
  https://www.nonprofitmaine.org/

- **Maryland**

  Maryland Nonprofits:
  https://www.marylandnonprofits.org/

- **Massachusetts**

  Massachusetts Nonprofit Network:
  http://massnonprofitnet.org/

- **Michigan**

  Michigan Nonprofit Association:
  https://mnaonline.org/

- **Minnesota**

  Minnesota Council of Nonprofits:
  https://www.minnesotanonprofits.org/

- **Mississippi**

  Mississippi Alliance of Nonprofits and Philanthropy:
  https://alliancems.org/

- **Missouri**

  Nonprofit Missouri:
  https://nonprofitmissouri.org/

- **Montana**

  Montana Nonprofit Association:
  https://www.mtnonprofit.org/

- **Nebraska**

  Nonprofit Association of the Midlands (serving Nebraska & Western Iowa):
  https://www.nonprofitam.org/page/advocacy

- **Nevada**

  Alliance for Nevada Nonprofits:
  https://alliancefornevadanonprofits.com/

- **New Hampshire**

  New Hampshire Center for Nonprofits:
  https://www.nhnonprofits.org/

- **New Jersey**

  NJ Center for Nonprofits:
  https://njnonprofits.org/

- **New Mexico**

  New Mexico Thrives:
  https://www.nmthrives.org/

- **New York**

  New York Council of Nonprofits:
  https://www.nycon.org/
  Nonprofit New York:
  https://www.nonprofitnewyork.org/

- **North Carolina**

  North Carolina Center for Nonprofits:
  https://www.ncnonprofits.org/

- **North Dakota**

  North Dakota Association of Nonprofit Organizations:
  https://www.ndano.org/about/leadership.html

- **Ohio**

  Ohio Association of Nonprofit Organizations:
  https://www.OANO.org

- **Oklahoma**

  Oklahoma Center for Nonprofits:
  https://okcnp.org/

- **Oregon**

  The Nonprofit Association of Oregon:
  https://nonprofitoregon.org/

- **Pennsylvania**

  Pennsylvania Association of Nonprofit Organizations:
  https://pano.org/

- **Rhode Island**

  Rhode Island Foundation:
  https://rifoundation.org/
  Rhode Island Department of State, Information for Non-Profit Corporations:
  https://www.sos.ri.gov/divisions/business-services/non-profit

- **South Carolina**

  Together SC:
  https://www.togethersc.org/

- **South Dakota**

  South Dakota Nonprofit Network:
  https://www.sdnonprofitnetwork.org/

- **Tennessee**

  Alliance for Better Nonprofits (East Tennessee):
  https://www.betternonprofits.org/
  Center for Nonprofit Management (Nashville/Middle Tennessee):
  https://www.cnm.org/
  Tennessee Secretary of State – How Do I Register a Nonprofit in
  Tennessee?:
  https://sos.tn.gov/businesses/faqs/how-do-i-register-a-nonprofit-in-tennessee

- **Texas**

  Texas Nonprofit Strong:
  https://txnonprofits.org/

- **Utah**

  Utah Nonprofits Association:
  https://utahnonprofits.org/

- **Vermont**

  Common Good Vermont:
  https://commongoodvt.org/about-us/
  The Vermont Community Foundation:
  https://vermontcf.org/nonprofits-and-grantseekers/

- **Virginia**

  Center for Nonprofit Excellence:
  https://www.thecne.org/

- **Washington**

  Nonprofit Association of Washington:
  https://nonprofitwa.org/

- **Washington, DC**

  Center for Nonprofit Advancement:
  https://www.nonprofitadvancement.org/

- **West Virginia**

  West Virginia Nonprofit Association:
  https://wvnpa.org/

- **Wisconsin**

  Wisconsin Nonprofits:
  https://wisconsinnonprofits.org/

- **Wyoming**

  Wyoming Nonprofit Network:
  https://www.wynonprofit.org/

# APPENDIX II –
# IRS 501 DISTINCTIONS

———··◉··———

| Type | Description | Contributions allowable? |
|---|---|---|
| 501(c)(1) | Corporations Organized under Act of Congress (including Federal Credit Unions) | Yes |
| 501(c)(2) | Title Holding Corporation for Exempt Organization | No |
| 501(c)(3) | Religious, Educational, Charitable, Scientific, Literary, Testing for Public Safety, to Foster National or International Amateur Sports Competition, or Prevention of Cruelty to Children or Animals Organizations | Yes |
| 501(c)(4) | Civic Leagues, Social Welfare Organizations, and Local Associations of Employees | No, generally* |
| 501(c)(5) | Labor, Agricultural, and Horticultural Organizations | No |
| 501(c)(6) | Business Leagues, Chambers of Commerce, Real Estate Boards, etc. | No |
| 501(c)(7) | Social and Recreational Clubs | No |
| 501(c)(8) | Fraternal Beneficiary Societies and Associations | Yes, if for certain Sec. 501(c)(3) purposes |
| 501(c)(9) | Voluntary Employees Beneficiary Associations | No |
| 501(c)(10) | Domestic Fraternal Societies and Associations | Yes |
| 501(c)(11) | Teachers' Retirement Fund Associations | No |
| 501(c)(12) | Benevolent Life Insurance Associations, Mutual Ditch or Irrigation Companies, Mutual or Cooperative Telephone Companies, and Like Organizations | No |
| 501(c)(13) | Cemetery Companies | Yes |
| 501(c)(14) | State-Chartered Credit Unions, Mutual Reserve Funds | No |
| 501(c)(15) | Mutual Insurance Companies or Associations | No |
| 501(c)(16) | Cooperative Organizations to Finance Crop Operations | No |

| Type | Description | Contributions allowable? |
| --- | --- | --- |
| 501(c)(17) | Supplemental Unemployment Benefit Trusts | No |
| 501(c)(18) | Employee Funded Pension Trust (created before June 25, 1959) | No |
| 501(c)(19) | Post or Organization of Past or Present Members of the Armed Forces | No, generally* |
| 501(c)(21) | Black Lung Benefit Trusts | No |
| 501(c)(22) | Withdrawal Liability Payment Fund | No |
| 501(c)(23) | Veterans' Organization (created before 1880) | No, generally* |
| 501(c)(25) | Title Holding Corporations or Trusts with Multiple Parent Corporations | No |
| 501(c)(26) | State-Sponsored Organization Providing Health Coverage for High-Risk Individuals | No |
| 501(c)(27) | State-Sponsored Workers' Compensation Reinsurance Organization | No |
| 501(c)(28) | National Railroad Retirement Investment Trust | No |
| 501(c)(29) | CO-OP health insurance issuers | No |
| | *See the IRS Publication 557 pages 68-70 for more details. | |

# APPENDIX III –
# BUSINESS PLAN*

———··●··———

## 1. Executive summary

The executive summary is an overview of your nonprofit and your plans. It is first in your business plan and is ideally only one to two pages. Most people write the summary last, summarizing all of the other sections.

The executive summary should be able to act as a stand-alone document that covers the highlights of your detailed plan. It should include your mission statement, goals, and objectives. It should also include an overview of the problem you are solving, the services you will offer, the goals you are trying to achieve, your target market, competition, and market strategy. List a handful of reasons why your organization will be successful, and talk about any successes already achieved. Depending on how far along you are in your process, you may also include a brief description of your team, a summary of your financials, and your funding requirements.

## 2. Nonprofit Overview

The Nonprofit Overview will give the details of your organization. This should include what type of corporation and the IRS 501 type of nonprofit you are (or expect to become), the physical location address, your mission statement, and the backstory of how, when, and why the organization was formed.

Include details about your team – management team members and board members. Describe their prior successes. (You may choose to include board member bios and an organizational chart showing the internal structure here or in the business plan appendices.) If there are gaps in your team, describe who you still need to cover those gaps. Describe any milestones the nonprofit has already reached.

## 3. Products & Services

Detail the need your organization will be covering and the plan to provide services to fill this need. Who is your target audience? Be as specific as possible as to age, gender, and other demographics. Explain how you plan to locate and reach this population. Discuss the size of the population that exists and how many of them your program aims to reach.

## 4. Operations Plan

This section spells out the day-to-day key operational processes. List the programs your nonprofit will be running, who will staff them (the personnel plan), where the programs will take place, and the expected cost to run them. There should be a timeline of expected milestones and a plan to measure success. Describe any products or additional services you plan to offer. Mention the resources you have, including facilities, funds, volunteers, and partnerships and how you plan to put them to use.

Next, discuss your longer-term plans for the organization. What impact do you expect to have had on the community in the next year? Include thoughts about running the existing programs in additional locations or your aspirations for adding programs.

You, as the founder of the organization, may want to discuss your plan for succession of the nonprofit. What is your plan as to turning it over to the board and (future) executive director to run, and when do you see yourself exiting?

## 5. Competitive Analysis

The Competitive Analysis section is where you talk about the direct and indirect competition to your organization. Make it clear that you have done your homework and are aware of the industry trends locally and elsewhere as well as the other resource organizations out there doing similar work. How do you plan to compete? Discuss what makes your nonprofit uniquely qualified to compete in this space, how you will offer the needed services, and how you will improve on what is being offered by the competition.

The competitive analysis chapter of your business plan can also be a good place to include a SWOT analysis. This is optional but can be a good way to explain how your products and services are positioned to deal with competitive threats and take advantage of opportunities.

## 6. Marketing

The marketing section of your business plan details your branding and how you intend to market your organization. You will be promoting your products, programs, and services to potential funders as well as to those who may need your services. Talk about your overall marketing strategies, which social media and other platforms you will use, and how you will measure the success of your outreach efforts.

Branding includes everything from your logo to the colors you will use consistently to represent your organization. If there is a specific reason you chose those colors, explain it here.

## 7. Financial Plan

Last, but possibly most important, is your financial plan chapter. This is often what people find most daunting, but it doesn't have to be as intimidating as it seems. Financials for most early-stage nonprofits are less complicated than you think, and a business degree is certainly not required to build a solid financial forecast. If you need additional help, there are plenty of tools and resources out there to help you build a solid financial plan.

In this section you want to answer the questions about your financial goals, where your funds will come from (do you have a plan to generate revenue in addition to soliciting donations?), and where and how they will be used. List funding you have in hand and lay out your projections for future funding. Look at similar nonprofits to get ideas of the funding they have received in your area.

Next, look at projected expenses. (See Chapter 8 in this book and the sample budget in Appendix VI to get an idea of what expenses you may incur.) List any key assumptions you have made about the market and industry in your forecast.

A typical financial plan will include:

- **Projected Income Statement**
  - A projected income statement is similar to a budget sheet listing the expected income and expenses with the net income (or loss) at the bottom. Include any depreciation, loan repayments, and other non-cash items. Project out for 2-3 years.

- **Balance Sheet**
  - A balance sheet provides a snapshot of your assets, liabilities, and equity at a given moment in time.

- **Cash Flow Statement** (include if already-existing nonprofit)
  - While the income statement calculates your profits and losses and includes some non-cash items, the cash flow statement keeps track of the inflows and outflows of cash in you accounts.

## 8. Appendix

An appendix to your business plan isn't a required chapter. However, it is a useful place to stick any charts, tables, definitions, legal notes, bios of board members, or other critical information that either felt too long or too out-of-place to include elsewhere in your business plan.

* A nonprofit business plan requires a lot of information. A good plan will be anywhere from 10 to 30 pages, or maybe more.

# APPENDIX IV –
# SAMPLE CERTIFICATE OF
# INCORPORATION/CHARTER

---

### CERTIFICATE OF INCORPORATION OF
### XYZ Charity, Inc.

XYZ Charity, Inc. (the "Corporation"), a charitable nonstock corporation organized and existing under the laws of the State of Delaware, hereby certifies that:

1. The present name of the corporation is XYZ Charity, Inc.
2. This Certificate of Incorporation of the Corporation was duly adopted in accordance with the provisions of Sections 242 and 245 of the General Corporation Law of the State of Delaware.

### ARTICLE I

The name of the Corporation is XYZ Charity, Inc.

### ARTICLE II

The registered address of the Corporation in the State of Delaware is 101 Main Street, Hometown, DE 12345. The name of the Corporation's registered agent at such address is Mary A. Smith.

The purpose of the Corporation is:

a. To operate exclusively for charitable, scientific, literary or educational purposes;
b. To receive and maintain a fund or funds of personal property, and, subject to the restrictions and limitations hereinafter set forth, to use and apply the whole or any part of the income therefrom and the principal thereof exclusively for charitable, scientific, literary, or educational purposes,

either directly or by contributions to organizations that qualify as exempt organizations under Section 501(c)(3) of the Internal Revenue Code of 1986, as amended as of the date hereof (the "Code").

c. To engage in any and all activities incidental to the foregoing purposes, except as specifically restricted herein.

The Corporation shall be a "charitable nonstock corporation" as defined in Section 114(d)(1) of the General Corporation Law of the State of Delaware and, as such, shall not be authorized to issue capital stock. The conditions of membership in the Corporation shall be set forth in the bylaws of the Corporation (the "Bylaws").

## ARTICLE III

At all times, and notwithstanding merger, consolidation, reorganization, termination, dissolution or winding up of the Corporation, voluntarily or involuntarily, or by operation of law or any other provision hereof:

a. No part of the net earnings of the Corporation shall inure to the benefit of any member, trustee, director or officer of the Corporation, or any private individual (except that reasonable compensation may be paid for services rendered to or for the Corporation affecting one or more of its purposes), and no member, trustee, director or officer of the Corporation, or any private individual, shall be entitled to share in the distribution of any of the corporate assets or the dissolution of the Corporation.

b. No substantial part of the activities of the Corporation shall consist of the carrying on of propaganda or otherwise attempting to influence legislation, and the Corporation shall not participate in or intervene in (including by publication or distribution of statements) any political campaign on behalf of (or in opposition to) any candidate for public office.

c. The Corporation shall not be operated for the purpose of carrying on a trade or business for profit.

d. The Corporation shall distribute its income for each taxable year at such time and in such manner as not to subject the Corporation to the tax on undistributed income imposed by Section 4942 of the Code.

e. The Corporation shall not engage in any act of self-dealing as defined in Section 4941 of the Code.

f. The Corporation shall not retain any excess business holdings as defined in Section 4943 of the Code.

g. The Corporation shall not make any investments in such a manner as to subject the Corporation to tax under Section 4944 of the Code.

h. The Corporation shall not make any taxable expenditures as defined in Section 4945 of the Code.

i. Notwithstanding any other provision of this certificate, the Corporation shall not conduct or carry on any activities not permitted to be conducted or carried on by an organization exempt under Section 501(c)(3) of Code, or by an organization contributions to which are deductible under Section 170(c)(2) of the Code.

j. Upon the dissolution of the Corporation or the winding up of its affairs, after paying or making provision for the payment of all liabilities and obligations of the Corporation, the assets of the Corporation shall be distributed exclusively to charitable, scientific, literary, or educational organizations which would then qualify under the provisions of Section 501(c)(3) of the Code.

## ARTICLE IV

The Corporation shall be financed through contributions, gifts, grants, donations, bequests, devises, benefactions and other voluntary transfers of property.

## ARTICLE V

The Corporation shall have perpetual existence.

## ARTICLE VI

The business and affairs of the Corporation shall be managed by or under the direction of the governing body of the Corporation. The governing body shall be known as the Board of Directors, and individual members of the Board of Directors shall be known as directors. The number of directors which shall constitute the whole board shall be fixed by the Board of Directors in the manner provided in the Bylaws, but in no event shall the number be less than three (3) or more than twenty-one (21).

Directors shall serve for terms ending at the third Annual Meeting after their election or appointment to the Board of Directors. Directors may serve for up to three successive three-year terms (for a total of nine successive years) and may be elected to further terms following a two-year break in service as a director; provided, however, that for purposes of calculating the number of years of service by any director, any period of time during which the director also serves as an officer of the Corporation, any period during which the immediate past President of the Corporation serves as an *ex-officio* member of the Board of Directors in accordance with the Bylaws of the Corporation and any period of less than six months between the time of appointment and the next Annual Meeting shall not be counted in determining eligibility to serve as a director. At each Annual Meeting, directors whose term expires at such Annual Meeting shall stand for reelection unless such director is not eligible for reelection due to exceeding the number of successive terms for which a director may be elected or due to failure to meet the qualifications set forth in the Bylaws. The Bylaws shall specify the number of directors necessary to constitute a quorum for the transaction of business at any meeting of the Board of Directors. Any director of the Corporation may be removed from office, with or without cause, by the affirmative vote of a majority of members of the Board of Directors present at any meeting thereof at which a quorum is present.

## ARTICLE VII

The Board of Directors shall have the power to make, adopt, amend or repeal, from time to time, the Bylaws.

## ARTICLE VIII

The members of the Corporation as such shall have no voting rights and no separate vote of members shall be required on any matter, except with respect to any matter where a member vote is required by law and such member vote cannot be eliminated by provision of the certificate of incorporation. If and to the extent that a vote of members is required by law on any matter and cannot be eliminated by provision of the certificate of incorporation, the vote of the Board of Directors shall be the vote of the members on such matters.

## ARTICLE IX

A director of the Corporation shall not be personally liable to the Corporation or its members for monetary liability for breach of fiduciary duty as a director, except for liability (i) for any breach of the director's duty of loyalty to the Corporation or its members, (ii) for acts or omissions not in good faith or which involved intentional misconduct or a knowing violation of law, or (iii) for any transaction from which the director derived an improper personal benefit.

## ARTICLE X

Upon dissolution of the Corporation, the Board of Directors shall: (a) pay or make provision for the payment of all the Corporation's liabilities; (b) return, transfer or convey (or make provision therefor) all assets held by the Corporation upon condition requiring such return, transfer or conveyance in the event of dissolution of the Corporation; and (c) dispose of the Corporation's remaining assets exclusively for the purposes of the Corporation or distribute the assets to an organization or organizations organized and operated exclusively for charitable, educational, scientific, religious, or literary purposes as shall, at that time, qualify for exemption under Section 501(c)(3) of the Code, as the Board of Directors shall determine; provided that none of such assets shall be distributed to any entity, fund or foundation any part of whose net earnings inures to the benefit of or is distributable to any individual or any entity for profit. Any such assets not so disposed of shall be disposed of by the circuit court of the city or county in which the principal office of the Corporation is then located, to be used exclusively for purposes that are charitable, educational, scientific, religious, or literary within the meaning of Section 501(c)(3) of the Code or to an organization or organizations organized and operated exclusively for such purposes.

## ARTICLE XI

The Corporation reserves the right to amend, alter or change any provision contained in this Certificate of Incorporation in the manner now or hereafter prescribed by applicable statute, and all rights conferred herein are granted subject to this reservation.

The undersigned duly authorized officer of XYZ Charity, Inc. has executed this Certificate of Incorporation on this 16th day of December 2020.

XYZ Charity, Inc.

By: Mary A. Smith
President

# APPENDIX V –
# SAMPLE ORG CHART

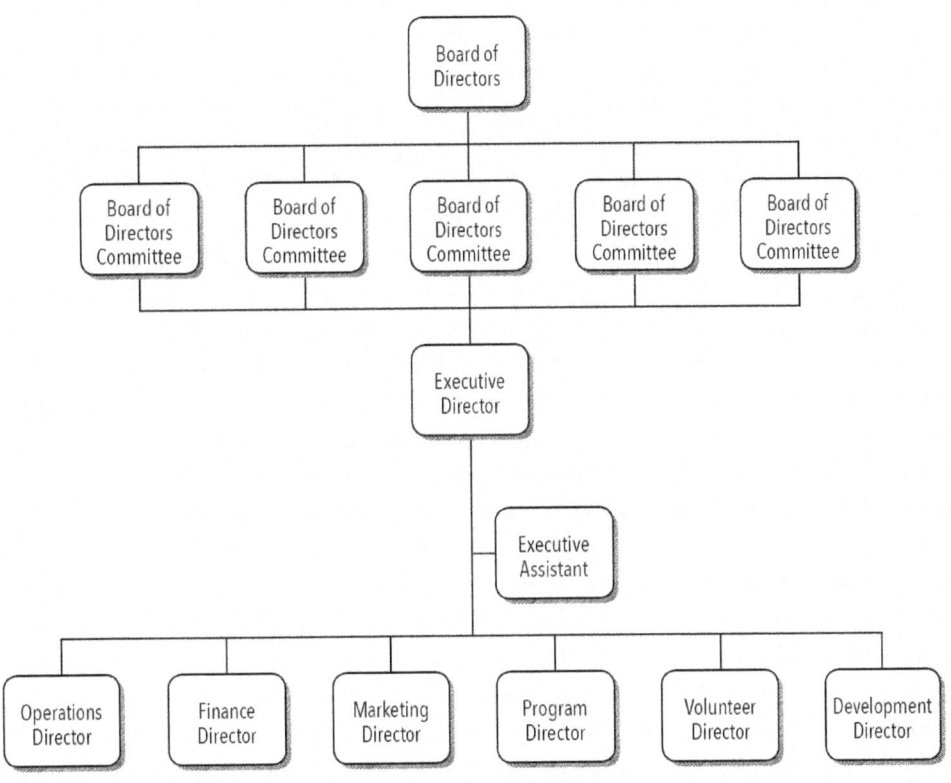

# APPENDIX VI – SAMPLE BUDGET

| XYZ Organization 7/1/2022 - 6/30/2023 | Budget 6/30/2023 | Actual Total To-Date 2/28/2023 | Actual to Budget % | Actual 6/30/2022 |
|---|---|---|---|---|
| **Income** | | | | |
| Annual Campaign | $ 15,000.00 | - | | $ 15,724.48 |
| Misc. Donations | 15,000.00 | 5,682.29 | 37.88% | 34,278.40 |
| Signature Event Income: | | | | |
| Sponsorship | 40,000.00 | 22,555.00 | 56.39% | 36,750.00 |
| Tickets | 15,000.00 | - | | - |
| Donations | 8,000.00 | 5,846.65 | 73.08% | 7,372.32 |
| Raffle | 4,500.00 | 6,330.00 | 140.67% | 3,540.00 |
| Grants | 40,000.00 | 32,649.57 | 81.62% | 54,108.94 |
| Interest Income | - | - | | - |
| Total Income | $ 137,500.00 | $ 73,063.51 | 53.14% | $ 151,774.14 |
| **Expenses** | | | | |
| Administrative Expenses: | | | | |
| Admin Services | 600.00 | 297.57 | 49.60% | 640.65 |
| Admin Supplies | 200.00 | 453.84 | 226.92% | 180.20 |
| Meeting Expense | - | - | | 750.00 |
| Franchise Tax Fee | 25.00 | - | | 25.00 |
| Post Office Box Fee | 146.00 | - | | 118.00 |
| Marketing & Communications: | 2,075.00 | 1,528.01 | 73.64% | 3,380.20 |
| Insurance: General Liability & Event | 772.00 | 772.00 | 100.00% | 772.00 |
| Insurance: D&O | 700.00 | 698.00 | 99.71% | 698.00 |
| Bank Fees | 50.00 | 65.95 | 131.90% | 20.00 |
| Zoom Account, Website | 180.00 | 119.92 | 66.62% | 164.89 |
| Total Administrative Expense | 4,748.00 | 3,935.29 | 82.88% | 6,748.94 |
| Event Expenses | 24,100.00 | 9,225.71 | 38.28% | 8,870.48 |
| Program Expenses | 95,172.00 | 87,465.99 | 91.90% | 86,732.29 |
| Fundraising Expenses | 2,350.00 | 1,259.93 | 53.6% | 2,249.69 |
| Database | 3,250.00 | 203.00 | 6.25% | 3,241.20 |
| Total Operating Expenses | 129,620.00 | 102,089.92 | 78.76% | 107,842.60 |
| Net Operating Income | $ 7,880.00 | $ (29,026.41) | | $ 43,931.54 |
| % Administrative Cost to Income | 3% | 5% | | 4% |

189

# APPENDIX VII –
# EVENT SPONSOR PACKET

A sponsorship packet, the information you give to prospective event sponsors, should be made up of four items. The final draft that you send out should be a PDF (to be sure the formatting does not change) of all pages in one document.

The first page should be a cover letter that is personalized to the prospect and signed by a board, staff, or committee member. If sending it in the mail, a hand-written note at the top is a nice personal touch. If emailing, write a short note in the body of the email explaining your attachment. The cover letter should detail why you need to raise funds, how previous funds have been spent and what great accomplishments they made possible, as well as the intention for funds you will raise with this event. The letter should be printed on your organization's letterhead with your logo. List board and advisory members and any other prominent members of your organization along the side or at the top.

Page two should be an 8 ½ x 11" version of the invitation with all event details. The next page or two will be the sponsorship levels – cost and benefits (like the type of publicity you guarantee and number of event tickets they will receive) for each level.

The last page is the sponsorship sign-up page. Be sure to add a contact phone or email for questions. You want to capture the following information:

- Company name (if applicable), contact name (person responsible within the organization), phone, email, and physical address
- Sponsorship level
- Payment details – provide a URL for them to pay online through your payment service OR credit card details if they are filling out a form (be sure to ask name on card, their contact information, card number, expiration, and CVV #).

# RESOURCES

————·•◉•·————

*S*o, *You Want to Start a Nonprofit, Now What?* and 501 Guide were developed as resources for all nonprofit organizations. The **501Guide.com** website provides access to additional nonprofit information, valuable tools, and sample bylaws and policy documents to keep your nonprofit running smoothly and successfully.

Michele Whetzel is a nonprofit consultant and may be reached through the website or by email at mlwhetzel@501Guide.com.

# ABOUT THE AUTHOR

**M**ichele Whetzel has worked in the nonprofit arena for more than 20 years, having served on more than a dozen boards and numerous committees. Over the years she has served in many different board positions, chairing events and heading annual campaign, grant, and governance committees. Her executive committee roles range from treasurer to board president/chair. The experience gained through her varied board work and nonprofit consulting gave Michele an extensive nonprofit education and viewpoint she believes could be a help to others.

As a facilitator, Michele proudly connects various people to other people and opportunities. She advocates for under-represented people to improve their lives and help get them a seat at the table. Michele has seen firsthand how ethical behavior and transparency, along with hard work and passion, lead to success.

She is continually learning and chooses to share what she has learned to help others reach success. Michele has a Bachelor of Science degree in Finance with a minor in Economics from the University of Delaware. She received her "Preparing to Be a Corporate Director" certification from Harvard Business School in fall 2020.

Michele lives with her husband, Robert, in Delaware when they are not traveling. They have two adult children who both live in Nashville, Tennessee.

Visit the website www.501Guide.com for more nonprofit information and access to sample bylaws and other documents.